M000196944

Euripides
Plays: Two

Hecuba, The Women of Troy, Iphigenia at Aulis, Cyclops

Euripides presents an unrelenting, painful cry against the waste of war. The three tragedies collected here illuminate both the enormity of war's processes as well as the unstoppable chain of individual tragedies such events engender. For all the agonies suffered by the protagonists these plays remain lyrical, stimulating and uplifting works, delivered here in clear, speakable translations. *Hecuba* is a play haunted by spirits, it shows how the snuffing out of decencies leaves a bitter aftertaste of the consuming destructiveness of war. *The Women of Troy* is a poem of pain, in which women of great strength and dignity are seen to suffer in the aftermath of a war in which they have become the victims. In *Iphigenia at Aulis* Agamemnon reacts to the prophecy that unless he sacrifices his daughter his expedition will be doomed to failure. His moral dilemma is complicated by circumstances and by the pressures of an army which does not want defeat. *Cyclops* is the only surviving comic afterpiece, known as a satyr play, offering both comic relief and a measure of reassurance. The volume is introduced by J. Michael Walton, series editor of the Methuen Classical Greek Dramatists.

Euripides was born near Athens between 485 and 480 BC and grew up during the years of Athenian recovery after the Persian Wars. His first play was presented in 455 BC and he wrote some hundred altogether. Nineteen survive – a greater number than those of Aeschylus and Sophocles combined – including *Alkestis, Medea, Bacchae, Hippolytos, Ion,* and *The Women of Troy.* His later plays are marked by a sense of disillusion at the futility of human aspiration which amounts on occasion to a philosophy of absurdism. A year or two before his death he left Athens to live at the court of the king of Macedon, dying there in 406 BC.

EURIPIDES

Plays: Two

Hecuba
translated by Peter D. Arnott

The Women of Troy
Iphigenia at Aulis
translated by Don Taylor

Cyclops
translated by J. Michael Walton

introduced by J. Michael Walton

series editor: J. Michael Walton

METHUEN DRAMA

METHUEN CLASSICAL GREEK DRAMATISTS

This edition first published in Great Britain in 1991
by Methuen Drama
Methuen Publishing Ltd
215 Vauxhall Bridge Road
London SW1V 1EJ

www.methuen.co.uk

Methuen Publishing Ltd reg. number 3543167

Hecuba first published in this translation in *Hecuba and the Madness of Herakles* by Macmillan Ltd, London and St. Martin's Press, New York, in 1969. Translation copyright © 1969, 1991 by Peter D. Arnott
The Women of Troy and *Iphigenia at Aulis* first published in this translation in *Euripides: The War Plays*, by Methuen Drama in 1990
Translation copyright © 1990, 1991 by Don Taylor
Cyclops translation copyright © 1991 by J. Michael Walton
Introduction copyright © 1991 by J. Michael Walton
This collection copyright © 1991 by Methuen Drama

The author and translators have asserted their moral rights

A CIP catalogue record for this book is available at the British Library

ISBN 0 41316420 9

Transferred to digital printing 2002

Caution

All rights whatsoever in these translations are strictly reserved. Application for amateur and professional performance, etc, should be directed before rehearsals begin, to: for *Hecuba*, to Methuen Publishing Ltd; for *The Women of Troy* and *Iphigenia at Aulis*, to Casarotto Ramsay Ltd, National House, 60-66 Wardour Street, London W1V 4ND; for *Cycolps*, to J. Michael Walton, Drama Department, University of Hull, Hull HU6 7RX. No performance may be given unless a licence has been obtained.

This paperback is sold subject to the condition that it shall not, by way of trade or otherwise, be lent, resold, hired out or otherwise circulated without the publisher's prior consent in any form of binding or cover other than that in which it is published and without a similar condition including this condition being imposed on the subsequent purchaser.

In Memory of Peter D Arnott
1931–1990

CONTENTS

INTRODUCTION

Of all the Greek playwrights, Euripides speaks most directly to a modern audience. The time when Greek drama seemed remote, something to admire from the security of the study, is passing as fast as are so many partial views fostered by the closeted scholarship of the late nineteenth and early twentieth centuries. If today there is an equal risk of treating the Athenian tragedians as though they belong to the age in which we live, the apparent modernity of the plays is returning them to the stage. There they are taking their rightful place, not as some precious oasis in an uncomfortable world, but as forceful reminders that the problems we face today are not new problems but old ones in a different mask.

I began work on this volume in Delphi during the first Theatrical Competition in Ancient Greek Drama for Young People. Nine European countries were represented, Denmark, Britain, France, Germany, Greece, Holland, Italy, Spain and Portugal. Some of the productions were professional, some amateur with companies of drama students soon to launch themselves into a profession where they must earn their living and where Greek plays have not often been regarded as good box-office. From the further corners of the building echoed a chorus of Dutch Bacchants, unlikely to take off in their frenzy over Parnassus, but prepared two days later to assert the rights and rites of Dionysus in the home of Apollo. Outside the window a modern Greek Agamemnon justified himself to his brother Menelaus in an early scene from *Iphigenia at Aulis*, one of the plays in the present volume seen recently in Don Taylor's television production.

The crickets were chattering and the tourist buses rumbling along the road below heading for the coast twenty kilometres away where the pilgrims used to land before winding their way up through the olive groves to consult the oracle. Delphi is still the special place it always was but it is not a place of escape, a place to forget the outside world. The oracle was consulted about the most important issues of the day: about war and alliances; about hostages and sanctuary; about deciding when and how to exert pressure on dictators; about learning when to talk and when the talking has to stop.

How appropriate that Delphi should aim to become a centre for the continuing revival of the Greek plays first performed in the Theatre of Dionysus in Athens in the fifth and fourth centuries BC. The festivals at Athens and Epidaurus have flourished for many years. What was exciting about the competition at Delphi was the desire of the young companies to apply a contemporary sensibility in terms of a theatrical vision cultivated in the drama of the twentieth century. This is not to underestimate the history of revival over the last hundred years. All over Europe and America, and recently in Japan too, classical plays have made a bid to return to the repertoire. But the impetus has been sporadic, confined often to individual enthusiasms, with reverence for the spoken word too often counting for more than a total theatrical experience. Not that Max Reinhardt could ever have been accused of merely paying homage to Aeschylus and Sophocles, but there must be a middle path between productions which make the plays appear moribund and some modern versions that render them invisible. Directors like Peter Stein and Ninagawa have in recent years begun to show that it is possible to create productions which will make an audience gasp through their virtuosity and impact but still demonstrate a trust in the craft of the playwrights themselves.

One of the rewarding features of the Delphic festival was that these young actors and actresses, designers and directors, all took it for granted that Greek plays will be as natural and vital a part of the work they do as the plays of Lope de Vega, Shakespeare and Molière, or modern classics: Pirandello, Brecht and Dario Fo. That 'old' need not mean 'old-fashioned' is not such a discovery. With reference to ancient drama it has still taken some discovering.

The range of plays attempted in the competition was revealing. No one risked an Aeschylus. There were two by Sophocles, and two by Euripides. Five comedies made up the list, four by Aristophanes and a Menander. This may largely have been chance. It may, on the other hand, have reflected a contemporary sense that comedy is the medium for the serious idea and a broader base for communication across a language barrier. Perhaps, though, it points to a truth about the Greek theatre which accounts for the presence of the four Euripides plays included in the present volume.

Only seven Aeschylus plays survive. Writing early in the fifth century BC when the links within a group submission were closer than they later became, Aeschylus regularly submitted a tetralogy, with the three tragedies effectively forming the three acts of a single play. All that remains from his considerable output are four single acts: *Persians*, *Seven Against Thebes*, *Suppliants* and *Prometheus Bound* and one 'full' tragedy, the *Oresteia* – *Agamemnon*, *Libation-Bearers* and *Eumenides*. But even the *Oresteia* is incomplete. The satyr play *Proteus* has not survived. Too little is known about it for anyone to do more than hazard a guess as to how *Proteus* fitted with the *Oresteia*. But fit it did. Tragedy was completed by comedy, but a special kind of comedy.

The same was true for Sophocles. Three of his plays, *Oedipus Tyrannus*, *Oedipus at Colonus* and *Antigone*, look as though they should form a trilogy. They cover consecutive episodes in the fortunes of the house of Laius. They do, that is, if presented in this order, but the plays were not written as consecutive. *Antigone* predates *Oedipus Tyrannus* by a probable sixteen years while *Oedipus at Colonus* was first performed in 401 BC, five years after Sophocles' death. The connected trilogy was no longer in fashion but some connection between a group of plays was normal and the playwright still offered a satyr play in conclusion. The other four plays of Sophocles (*Ajax*, *Women of Trachis*, *Electra* and *Philoctetes*) are simply a representative sample of the playwright's work over thirty-five years. There is a bonus, though, in the case of Sophocles. About half survives of another play, the *Ichneutae*, usually translated as *The Searchers* or *The Trackers*. What makes this special is that *Ichneutae* is a satyr play.

In 1907 about four hundred lines of the play came to light at Oxyrinchus in Egypt. The significance to scholars was less the quality of the text than the comparison it offered to the one

satyr play which has survived in its entirety: Euripides' *Cyclops*.
For theatre practitioners *Ichneutae* seemed to offer little to
enthuse over, though there was a production at the theatre in
Syracuse in 1927 alongside the *Cyclops*.

In 1988 Tony Harrison, translator of the *Oresteia* which Sir
Peter Hall directed at the National Theatre in 1981, took the
remains of *Ichneutae* and wrote them into a piece of his own
which featured as leading characters Grenfell and Hunt, the
two scholars who discovered and deciphered the Sophocles
papyrus. Harrison's *The Trackers of Oxyrinchus* was first performed in Delphi as a joint production of the National Theatre
Studio and the European Cultural Centre of Delphi.

The original *Ichneutae* cannot be tied to any Sophocles play
or group of plays. This leaves open the question of how and
why a satyr play should have been considered an appropriate
appendix to tragic performance. Why should comedy follow
tragedy? How strong was the link? Titles that can be tied to
specific tragic diets suggest that the satyr play mocked ideas
and themes that were part of the tragedies. The satyr play to
Aeschylus' Theban tetralogy, which dealt with the story of
Oedipus and concluded with the extant *Seven Against Thebes*,
was *The Sphinx*, presumably some account of the creature
Oedipus defeated before becoming King of Thebes. What was
the link between the serious and the ludicrous?

That tragedy should be serious, or *spoudaios*, is confirmed
by Aristotle in his famous definition in the *Poetics*:

> Tragedy is the representation of an action which is worthy
> of concern (*spoudaios*), complete in itself and of some
> substance . . . by creating pity and fear causing the purga-
> tion (*katharsis*) of such emotions.
>
> Aristotle *Poetics* VI 2

Are we perhaps to assume that in the satyr play, however
ribald, however absurd, there is an element that is 'worthy of
concern', as necessary for *katharsis* as pity or fear? Is laughter
less an antidote to tragedy than a part of it, part of a process of
disengagement from a world that requires balance for
wholeness?

By the time of Euripides, any link between the four plays of a group submission was, at best, thematic. *Cyclops* cannot be dated, but its inclusion with *Hecuba, The Women of Troy* and *Iphigenia at Aulis* aims at an appraisal of the satyr play through the Trojan War theme which links these tragedies. They do not form a trilogy any more than do the Theban plays of Sophocles. They are simply three of the nineteen surviving plays of Euripides which use the aftermath of the Trojan defeat to reflect the playwright's changing attitude to the war through which he was living. *Hecuba* is the earliest of the three, performed about 425 BC. The Peloponnesian War between Athens and Sparta had already lasted for six years but sporadically. The threat of total destruction was one that could still be reserved for other people. This did not mean that Athenians and their allies were not being killed and maimed on the battlefield.

All the plays of the period question the conduct of war and often the need for it. The messages of Aristophanes and Euripides were hardly cryptic: 425 BC was the year in which Aristophanes presented *Acharnians* in which an ordinary Athenian, Dicaeopolis, is so tired of the war that he makes a private peace with the Spartans. During the course of the action Dicaeopolis breaks out of character and addresses the audience as though he were Aristophanes. Perhaps, indeed, the actor was Aristophanes. He reminds the audience of the play he had presented the previous year, *Babylonians*, which led to a criminal charge after he had mocked the Assembly for changing its policy on successive days. *Babylonians* had been presented at the Great Dionysia, too public an occasion for such pointed satire.

The incident to which Aristophanes had referred and which got him into hot water was one to which Euripides may well have been pointing, though more obliquely, in *Hecuba* from the same year as *Acharnians*. In 428 BC Mytilene, on the island of Lesbos, had revolted against her position under Athenian domination in the Delian confederacy. The Athenians responded by besieging the town and forcing the Mytileneans into submission. The Assembly in Athens promptly voted for the execution of the male population and the enslavement of all women and children. A warship was dispatched to carry out the people's will. Overnight, passions cooled and the following day the decision was reversed. Another and fortunately faster ship was sent to countermand the order and only the ring-leaders of the rebellion were put to death.

The dramatic festivals of 425 BC presented plays to an audience who might have suffered wounds or lost relatives at Mytilene or in other engagements. Some of them might have been on one of those two ships that set out for Mytilene. Many of them must have taken part in the successive days' voting.

Old Comedy, in the person of Aristophanes, had its serious dimension. It could be direct, forceful and dangerous. It was nothing like the satyr play, though, which clearly had a different function. The whole purpose of the satyr play has never been satisfactorily explained. The usual verdict has been that it provided comic relief but this is far too general a notion to account for a dramatic form which, in the work of Aeschylus, Sophocles and Euripides was a major part of a tragic dramatist's creative output. It may well be that a play such as *Cyclops*, for all its comic spine, is as 'worthy of concern' or *spoudaios*, as the tragedies themselves. If so, then it is likely that the nature of Dionysus will hold the clues to the enduring appeal of his attendant satyrs.

Dionysus was the god of many things as well as being god of the theatre. Lord of the disruptive and the uncomfortable, he stands for the theatre's right to probe and aggravate. If the Athenians could make themselves look foolish to others by the decisions they made over Mytilene, then Dionysus set up the mirror in which they saw their folly reflected. Aristophanes, writing plays that were partially set in the Athens of his day, could offer a reflection distorted, but recognisable as in a fairground hall of mirrors. Euripides turned the reflection into art with metaphor replacing realism. The theatre for him was a place in which to expose the pointlessness of all war and uncover the motives that masquerade as heroism.

Sometimes it seems that Euripides wrote out of his own mood. The surviving tragedies contain variations of many kinds. When his work includes the romantic *Helen*, the heart-wrenching *Heracles* and the vicious *Orestes*, there should be no problem accepting him as author of *Cyclops*. Only the categories of play were prescribed in Athens. Tragedy was tragedy, satyr was satyr and comedy was comedy. One group of playwrights wrote tragedies and satyrs, another group, comedies. There is some suggestion that a tragedian might get help in the writing of the satyr plays but not from a writer of Old Comedy. One play of Euripides does survive which reinforces the tragedy/satyr link. *Alcestis* was presented in the satyr position in 438 BC without being a satyr play. It tells the story of the King of Pherae, Admetus, who was granted the favour by Apollo that when his time came to die he could nominate a substitute. When the time does come, only his wife Alcestis is prepared to take his place. Soon after she dies Heracles arrives and is offered hospitality by Admetus who decides not to tell him of Alcestis' death. Heracles discovers the truth when reproved by a servant for carousing in a house of mourning. He promptly departs to wrestle with Death and returns with a veiled figure whom he eventually reveals to Admetus as the wife he believes he has lost. Charming story though it may be, *Alcestis* defies any attempt to label it as 'prosatyric'. It is simply a new kind of play, with a happy end and no obvious outlet in the festival structure. Rather than emphasising the difference between tragedy and satyr, *Alcestis* reinforces the link between the first three plays in a submission and the fourth.

Alcestis is admittedly an exception even amongst the spread to be found in Euripides which includes several plays which look forward to New Comedy rather than back to the grim worlds of Aeschylus and Sophocles. Some of the more savage plays do contain a comic side as grotesque and grisly as that to be found in much Jacobean tragedy. The war plays are unrelenting. *Hecuba*, *The Women of Troy* and *Iphigenia at Aulis* offer a particular perspective on the progress of the Peloponnesian War, from the anxieties in the wake of Mytilene to the desperation after a similar incident ten years on involving the island of Melos. Ten years again and with the Athenian defeat imminent, *Iphigenia at Aulis* was first presented to an audience which must have greeted Euripides' words as a message from the grave.

Hecuba is a play of ghosts. Polydorus, Hecuba's son, delivers the prologue. He is a wraith 'unmourned, unburied' who knows in death what the future holds for his sister and his mother. He has frightened Hecuba in a dream and is aware of the power a ghost may have to influence the present and the future. Another ghost, the ghost of the dead hero Achilles, has demanded that the Greeks sacrifice Polyxena before they set out for home. The audience never sees the ghost of Achilles and, after the prologue, Polydorus reappears only as a corpse under a sheet. The twin presences, spectres not only of men but of the power of the past, still haunt every moment of every ensuing scene.

The sacrifice demanded by Achilles' ghost is not irresistible whatever the arguments of Odysseus and 'Theseus' sons, twin scions of Athens' (line 125). Euripides is not pointing to the kind of decision that faces Agamemnon in *Iphigenia at Aulis*. When Aeschylus referred in his *Agamemnon* to the pressure on Agamemnon to sacrifice his daughter, the whole expedition hung upon his decision. It was a straight choice: sacrifice and go to Troy or fail to sacrifice and go home. Aeschylus' Agamemnon bowed before 'the yoke of Necessity', the necessity to make a choice, but the Necessity beyond man's control which had decided that war was inevitable. For Euripides, all such decisions are human decisions, dictated by self-interest, by circumstance or by blood-lust. So it proves to be in *Iphigenia at Aulis*. In *Hecuba* the army is divided about whether they should take any notice of Achilles' ghost. The ghosts in *Hecuba* can influence but it is the living who make the decisions and invoke the dead to justify what they want to do.

This is precisely what happens to Hecuba who turns from a *mater dolorosa*, barely capable of standing on her own two feet, to a killer for whom the murder of children and the maiming of Polymestor are the last pleasures left. Difficult as it is to avoid savouring the detestable Polymestor's undoing, the after-taste is of the consuming destructiveness of war.

What *Hecuba* demonstrates most clearly is the snuffing out of decencies. Hecuba has a scene with Odysseus in which she reminds him of the time when she recognised him in Troy on a spying mission. She saved him and allowed him to escape. When she asks for a life in return, the life of her daughter, he brushes her off, rather proud at how he has managed to talk himself out of an awkward situation. That is the private individual saving his skin. Then the politician takes over, the public man with his reasoned argument:

It's detrimental to the public interest
For a hero who has volunteered his life
To have no more reward than a deserter. (lines 306-8)

The play is full of such justifications, vile men with filthy excuses, but such plausible ones, for vile actions. Polymestor, guilty of murdering the boy sent into his protection, admits to being a neutral in the war but accounts for what he has done:

I feared if this boy lived to fight again
He might build a new Troy, and reunite its people;

(lines 1138-9)

. . . it would not be healthy then
To be Troy's neighbour. (lines 1143-4)

None of it is true. Polymestor killed Polydorus for the money.

Agamemnon is not much better, putting on airs about his civilisation as he offers condolences for Polydorus' death but disassociates himself from any fuller response:

In the name of justice and the gods, I wish
I could punish your perjuring friend for you.
If there were some way you could have your wish
Without the army thinking I had worked
The death of Polymestor for Cassandra's sake! (lines 852-6)

Hecuba sums up the world she sees in lines that smack as much of the playwright himself as of the character he has created, dismissing each man as

. . . a slave to his purse-strings, a slave to fortune,
Or public opinion or the force of law (lines 865-6)

When Agamemnon returns to the scene in response to Polymestor's screams he has the gall to pretend shock on discovering what the women have done.

Integrity is reserved for Polyxena who accepts her death, as Iphigenia accepts hers in *Iphigenia at Aulis*, but with no sense that her sacrifice has any purpose. A young girl is slaughtered to appease a ghost. Nothing is gained. Nothing is achieved. The foolishness and the waste drown out any other sentiment.

The Women of Troy has obvious points of contact with *Hecuba*. Some critics have felt the two plays to be so close that *The Women of Troy* is no more than a rewrite of *Hecuba*, but this underestimates both plays. The structure of *Hecuba* is more conventional, linking the story of the two children through the presence of the mother and building logically to the explosion of calculated revenge against the only target Hecuba can reach. *The Women of Troy* is built in a different way with a shape which has no parallel, I believe, in serious drama.

Athenian success in the early part of the war against Sparta and the uneasy stand-off, which had held since the signing of the Peace of Nicias in 421 BC, was the result of naval strength. The Athenian army was no match for the Spartans whose whole education system was geared to creating fighting men. Athens had always been a sea power. In war her authority depended on control of the islands. Most of those in the Aegean had become, perforce, part of the Delian confederacy, effectively the Athenian empire in the years that followed the Persian invasions of Greece in 490 and 480 BC. Taxes, in money or kind, were a guarantee of Athenian protection should the Persian threat ever return. As it became clear while Aeschylus was still alive that a new Persian offensive was about as likely as an attack by Harpies, the position of the subject-allies was called into question. Most of them felt more like subjects than allies and resented seeing their annual contribution deposited in the treasury at Delos and then apparently used to build the Parthenon or glorify the city of Athens with statues in silver and gold. They were not in any position to do more than grumble and the odd Mytilene ensured that grumbles never became concerted.

Some islands had managed to resist the pressure to become involved in the war between Athens and Sparta. One of those which proclaimed neutrality was Melos, whose case was heard in Athens and reported, apparently verbatim, by the historian Thucydides. The Athenians remained unconvinced by the

Melian claim to be left alone and besieged the city, in 416 BC; starving the Melians into submission. This time the Assembly had no second thoughts. No fast ship set out to countermand the orders of the previous day. The men were killed, the women and children sold into slavery. After an indecently short lapse, a group of 'new Melians' was sent out from Athens to colonise the deserted island. At the Great Dionysia follow-ing, Euripides presented a group of Trojan plays, *Alexander* (that is, Paris, whose abduction of Helen was the cause of the war), *Palamedes* (about the Greek warrior stoned to death at Troy after being suspected of spying for the Trojans), *The Women of Troy* and the satyr play *Sisyphus*.

It is inconceivable that the audience for the 415 BC produc-tion of *The Women of Troy* could have failed to relate what they saw on stage to the destruction of Melos. The Trojan War was an unavoidable metaphor for the Peloponnesian War through which they were living. Euripides' feelings touched nerves already fraying with the conflicting demands of nationalism and family affection. *Hecuba* and *The Women of Troy* are crammed with arguments for expediency in the cause of which people get killed.

The play opens with a prologue involving the two gods Poseidon and Athene, traditionally at loggerheads since Athene, rather than Poseidon, became patron of Athens. Poseidon appears first, the god who founded Troy and built the city with his own hands. Polyxena, he informs the audience, is already dead but Hecuba has not yet been told. The Greeks are on the point of leaving for home. All that remains is to parcel out the women reserved for the Greek leaders. Athene and Poseidon agree to join forces to punish the Greeks and make their homecoming as painful as possible. Athene may be the patron goddess of Athens but on this occasion she is siding with her enemy, outraged at an act of sacrilege. In 415 BC the Athenians were about to renew hostilities in earnest with the massive and expensive expedition, not against Sparta at all, but all the way to Sicily on a fool's errand that was to lose them an entire fleet.

A prologue between gods as an exposition scene recalls Euripides' first play, *Alcestis*. There too the gods make only one entrance. The difference in *The Women of Troy* is that after the departure of Athene and Poseidon, there is virtually no more drama. No drama in the expected sense, that is, for *The Women of Troy* proves in performance to be as searing an indictment of war as has ever been written for the stage. Conventional dramatic structure goes by the board. There are no real conflicts, no changes of direction. All that happens is that things get worse for Hecuba. She finds that she has been awarded to the hated Odysseus. She discovers that one of her daughters, Cassandra, is to become Agamemnon's whore and the poor crazed creature is brought onto the stage. Hecuba's daughter-in-law, Andromache, widow of Hector, is fetched in with her child Astyanax. Andromache tells Hecuba that Polyxena has been sacrificed. She has been allocated to Achilles' son Neoptolemus. Talthybius, the herald, arrives to take away Astyanax, condemned to death as a potential threat.

What more can be added to the sum of Hecuba's grief? Euripides has more. As the child is dragged away, Menelaus arrives with Helen, the cause of the entire war. Here, perhaps, is someone from whom Hecuba can exact retribution for all that she has suffered, as the Hecuba in *Hecuba* blinded Polymestor and exacted vengeance, child for child. But no, Euripides will allow no relief, simply the frustration of seeing Menelaus' passionate anger begin to dissolve into passion of another sort from which Helen will again emerge as a winner. Helen's defence of her position as a helpless victim of her beauty and of the gods has the initial plausibility of all of the Greeks when engaged in argument. They are all wonderful at justifying anything that they have done, Agamemnon and Polymestor in *Hecuba*, Talthybius and Helen in *The Women of Troy*. Euripides makes sure that the real motives shine through, ever pragmatic, but no more honourable for that.

The concluding scene of *The Women of Troy* offers no climax in the accepted dramatic sense, simply the parade of misery concentrated into the poignant image of the dead child returned on his father's shield. Andromache and Astyanax are introduced into the action on top of a cart loaded with booty. A few bits and pieces are salvaged at the end to give the boy some sort of funeral. His mother is no longer present, only the grandmother who now sees all hope of a future for her race stripped away. The final act is the firing of the city before the conquerors leave, oblivious of the destruction the twin gods have already prepared for them.

At first sight *The Women of Troy* seems less a play than a poem of pain. What gives the writing its dramatic power is a combination of features which belong wholly in a theatre. War is presented in its aftermath and almost exclusively through the eyes of the women who are its victims. The male characters are a hostile god, an apologetic herald, a cuckold and a child. Only the women have any strength, but they are the ones who suffer. They suffer corporately as a chorus, individually as Cassandra and Andromache, but all is condensed in the figure of Hecuba. Ten years previously Euripides had given Hecuba the power of resistance in a revenge, however futile. The Hecuba of 415 BC is impotent.

The play achieves greatness in the quality of its image. As an example of any and every war it transcends Trojans and Greeks, Athenians and Melians. Like Picasso's *Guernica* or Britten's *War Requiem*, *The Women of Troy* is a primal statement. The statement is itself composed of a series of smaller statements, about slavery and power, about callousness, stupidity, desperation and despair. Central is Hecuba herself but the change of title from the earlier play has a purpose. Personal disasters in the teeth of losing her country and her status have made of Hecuba an icon of suffering for future generations. The title *The Women of Troy* universalises her fate, making it applicable as long as men go to war. The acts of bravado, the massacres justified and the pettiness of the root causes provide running themes for play after play of Euripides. His attempts to cajole his fellow Athenians into seeing war's futility were no more effective than those of Aristophanes to have his philosophy taken seriously.

If *The Women of Troy* is the masterpiece, a personal cry of outrage at the atrocity of Melos, *Hecuba* is still a major work in its own right. Far from being the dummy run for *The Women of Troy* that some have dubbed it, *Hecuba* touches different nerves and raises its own disturbing questions about revenge and the placing of blame. *Iphigenia at Aulis* takes a new direction altogether, no afterthought but a cogent statement on how small deceptions snowball.

The action of *Iphigenia* precedes that of the other plays by ten years though it was not performed until the year after Euripides' death in Macedon. The old man had spent his declining years away from Athens but a group of last plays, amongst which are *Iphigenia at Aulis* and the *Bacchae*, were produced by his son and won first prize at tne Great Dionysia of 405 BC. Whether the *Iphigenia at Aulis* was written at the end of his life or was an earlier, unperformed play is a question beyond answer. Instinct suggests that it is not a haphazard piece, however curious a bedfellow for the *Bacchae*, but a final statement about war born of the distance of age and physical dislocation.

The Women of Troy shows the despair at the end of a war. *Iphigenia at Aulis* investigates how wars begin in the first place. The war is, as ever, the Trojan War, but a Trojan War that is nearer than ever to home. The Greek heroes have travelled a long way from Aeschylus' supermen. They display not only feet but heads of clay. In his introduction to *The War Plays* (Methuen, 1990), and in his television production, Don Taylor stressed the need for an interpretation in performance. Most of Euripides' plays contain the ambiguity of art which allows for alternatives according to production circumstance. A Greek production of the *Iphigenia* in the competition chose to emphasise the way in which Agamemnon only began to reject humanity as he took on the apparel of authority. The set featured a double bed with a blood-red cloth across it, simultaneously illustrating the blighted marriage and pre-figuring Agamemnon's return home in Aeschylus. Though Taylor has claimed that a translator must commit himself to a single viewpoint, I believe he underestimates the flexibility of his work.

In one respect I am in complete agreement with him. The scholarly arguments about the authenticity of parts of the text appear almost wilful in their disregard of the requirements of performance. Perhaps such a verdict is too harsh. There are corruptions in the text which appear to offer two opening scenes and many critics have been upset by the ending.

Posthumous work and 'bottom-drawer' plays often benefit from revision. Had such revision been accorded to the notes that have survived as Aristotle's *Poetics*, we might have had a clearer picture of the history of Greek drama and its aesthetics. It must be doubtful, though, if Aristotle would have revised his opinion of the *Iphigenia at Aulis*, which is unflattering. Iphigenia he singles out as inconsistent (*Poetics* XV 9) 'because Iphigenia as a suppliant is unlike her later self'. True enough, she pleads to Agamemnon for her life in a speech which is the more touching for its lack of concentrated eloquence. In *Hecuba*, *The Women of Troy* and elsewhere in *Iphigenia at Aulis*, the characters claim reasons for what they want to do by arguments that are largely specious, thought up to justify actions which different and darker motives dictate. Iphigenia says what she means, invoking her love for her father and her love of life.

Later in the play she accepts her position as sacrificial victim. What is interesting in production is the process that induces the transformation, a process treated entirely differently, as it happens, in Don Taylor's production and in the Greek production in the Delphi competition. Each solution was plausible, true to the text and, in the way that it placed emphasis on Agamemnon, demonstrated how what may seem a problem to an Aristotle is resolved on stage. A change of heart, such as Iphigenia's, may be perturbing, moving or simply romantic. It is not inconsistent. In this the shape of the play matches her attitude to that of other characters, notably Achilles, who confronts the army, confident in his power, only to discover that he has no influence at all over soldiers keyed up by bloodlust. Iphigenia's speech in which she claims the right to be a victim and readily submits to martyrdom is extraordinary. The childishness of her early exchanges with mother and father have developed into a submission in its way no less innocent. Far from being inconsistent, this is a part of the whole pattern of good intention which makes of the *Iphigenia*, not the harrowing document that is *The Women of Troy*, but a tragic exposé of people overtaken by events.

Time and again in *Iphigenia at Aulis* the leading characters attempt to make the best of a bad job. Agamemnon has accepted that he should be commander of the forces against

Troy because he is Menelaus' brother and for no other reason. When he hears of Calchas' prophecy that the expedition will never proceed without the sacrifice of Iphigenia, he first orders the army to be disbanded. Persuaded by Menelaus that he has to proceed, he devises the stratagem of the proposed marriage to Achilles as the only way to get Clytemnestra to bring Iphigenia to Aulis. In the opening scene as we have it here, a scene which carries dramatic conviction as it stands, Agamemnon has changed his mind again and sent a second letter. Menelaus intercepts it and argues the case for war with all the brash selfishness of the warrior-bullies Euripides has created in so many other plays. News arrives that Clytemnestra and Iphigenia have landed.

What happens next is a major turning-point in the play. Agamemnon argues his case so well that Menelaus confesses himself convinced by what his brother has to say. Agamemnon is right and no expedition, no war, is worth a daughter's life. But Menelaus is too late. The crucial mistakes have been made and the army has got wind of the sacrifice. One of the reasons for introducing Achilles is to show how the leaders have lost control and the mob must be appeased. The meeting of Achilles and Clytemnestra is one of pure embarrassment as she claims him as a son-in-law when he is the one person who has heard nothing of Agamemnon's plans. Typically, in this world of evasions and half-truths, it is the Old Man, part of Clytemnestra's dowry but now in Agamemnon's retinue, who reveals to the queen the intended murder of her daughter.

The sense of trying to do what is right accounts too for the attitude of Clytemnestra which, on the surface, is every bit as contrary as that of Iphigenia. Agamemnon, we hear later in the play, killed her former husband and murdered her child. All this notwithstanding, she has tried to be a 'model wife', welcoming her daughter's arranged marriage and, with a nice ironic touch, introducing the baby Orestes to the events which he is too young to comprehend but which will form his adult life.

The miraculous ending to *Iphigenia at Aulis*, with Iphigenia rescued in the nick of time like Isaac, can take a number of interpretations from divine intervention to downright deception. The restoration of received myth is used effectively by

Euripides in *Electra* and *Orestes* to point to the differences between the known story and his own dramatic version. The one thing that Euripides did not need to do was provide an ending which would be compatible with his having earlier written an *Iphigenia in Tauris* about the preserved Iphigenia being rescued by her brother Orestes many years hence. Though the outlines of myth were fixed, all manner of variations were possible from play to play.

More important is the tone of the whole play and the way it reveals an insight into Euripides late in his life. Age and distance from his home city that now faced total defeat lend a different dimension to the playwright's revelation. Too old to teach or to expect his audiences to learn, he can only use his experience to reflect on how human tragedy can develop from small errors of judgement as much as from the grosser follies. The outcome is no less horrific and the subtler vision is as terrifying as the directness of *Hecuba* or *The Women of Troy*.

Against this grim trio of plays from the most civilised of ancient cities in its most civilised of centuries, must now be set the deflecting force of the satyr play. The satyr play which followed *The Women of Troy* was *Sisyphus*, anticipating the absurdist vision of the futility of life by over two thousand three hundred years. Being dead was hell enough for heroes but the grand villains met with grand fates. Sisyphus had chained up Death and was to spend eternity pushing a stone towards a goal he would never reach. The idea must have appealed to Euripides. What better comment could there be on the fate of the didactic playwright?

Cyclops, the one surviving satyr play, is less philosophical in theme but affords the only opportunity we have to test the function of the satyr play against a text. At one level, and not a negligible one, the satyr play offers reassurance. Greek tragedies may be stimulating, moving and uplifting. They also tend to be hard work. Relief is rare in Aeschylus or Sophocles, though more common in Euripides. Any humour to be found in the more sombre plays is bitter or cruel. The Greek tragedians were well aware of dramatic rhythm and the importance of balancing mood and character but, unlike most drama since, Greek tragedy offers a directness which concentrates on the main issues and employs the chorus where dramatists of a later period took to the sub-plot or to comic interlude.

The place for comedy with a serious purpose was well enough appreciated by Homer for whom the gods were often the butt. In Athens of the fifth century the plays of Aristophanes and his contemporaries could propose the most pointed of political statements played off against the wildest of fantasies. Aristophanes' brush with Cleon which led to his defence of himself through the mouth of Dicaeopolis in *Acharnians* was not to prevent him writing in *Knights* one of the most *ad hominem* attacks in all drama. His mockery of the long-dead Aeschylus and the recently deceased Euripides in *Frogs* leads to a scurrilous competition over who is the better playwright, only resolved when each gives his opinion on the crucial political issue of the day. Laughter as relief at the end of the festival, or as a sly means of pointing to unpalatable truths, was well catered for in Old Comedy. The satyr play must have had a different purpose. It certainly had a longer pedigree.

Satyrs were attendants of the god Dionysus, theriomorphic entities with bald heads and pointed ears. They sported horses' tails and, in art, spend happy hours, usually with erections of Aubrey Beardsley proportions, chasing, and not infrequently catching up with, assorted nymphs and bacchants. Not that this was the extent of their taste. When the mood took them, not much that moved was safe and most of the time the mood took them. That the kind of sporty activity they represent should precede tragedy as a dramatic form is less surprising than that the satyr play should have had such staying power. In one form or another it lasted into the Christian era.

What resemblance Euripides' *Cyclops* might have had to any satyr piece from five hundred years later must be pure conjecture, but there is nothing to suggest that the form grew any more refined with the passing of Euripides: perhaps the reverse when the tragic plays no longer provided a context. The fixed elements were those that were least likely to be enshrined in print. As attendants of Dionysus, satyrs represented the baser side of the spirit of freedom, nature in the raw, drink and release from care and the customary restraints.

Dionysus became in time the god of the theatre, the satyr play a fixed part of a playwright's tragic submission. The god may not appear in person in *Cyclops*, as he does in Aristophanes' *Frogs* and Euripides' *Bacchae*, but Silenus and his chorus were there as his representatives in each and every satyr play. A long list of surviving titles and occasional fragments and quotations suggest a direct link between the tragedies and their afterpiece. Apart from Aeschylus' *The Sphinx*, Sophocles' *Ichneutae* and Euripides' *Sisyphus* and *Cyclops*, other titles point to the presence of Achilles, Helen, Heracles, Circe, Nausicaa and a host of others.

The direct link in proposing *Cyclops* as the satyr play to *Hecuba* must first be at the level of parody, *hilarotragodia*, as it is described in the Suda Lexicon, or, in modern theatre parlance, a 'send-up'. Each of the playwrights submitted three 'serious' plays, followed by a fourth whose tone was farcical but dealt with similar ideas. This, it would seem, was as true for Sophocles as for Euripides while Aeschylus had the reputation in classical times of writing the rudest and crudest satyr plays of all.

Cyclops certainly contains parody and is at base a simple farce, but a close look suggests that it may amount to more than the sum of its parts. Half the length of a tragedy or old comedy, it features Silenus and the satyrs in an incident which is not really anything to do with them, but is based on Book IX of Homer's *Odyssey*. The Homeric story is more adventure than comedy with any humour confined to the trick which Odysseus plays on Polyphemus when he tells him that his name is 'Nobody'. The rest is gruesome, with graphic descriptions of how Odysseus' men are killed. Euripides gives a dramatic substance which is comic, but which also supplies hints as to how the play may have been performed and why it was more than an afterpiece to send the audience away happy.

The two central figures are Odysseus and the Cyclops, Polyphemus. The plot follows the Homeric outline with a certain licence for what can or cannot easily be staged. Odysseus' men walk out of the cave after the blinding rather than hanging underneath the bellies of giant sheep. It is the chorus of satyrs who set the tone of the play as something laughable.

The quality of the language is higher than might be expected. The satyrs resort to double-entendres and colloquialisms but Odysseus maintains a formality. On only one occasion does he resort to slang and then he is quoting Polyphemus. Mostly he presents a sort of earnest heroism which falters at the end of a speech or of a dialogue exchange. The Messenger speech in which he describes the death of two of his companions inside the cave bears the stamp of the writer who could describe so passionately the mangling of Hippolytus or the frenzy of Heracles. Right at the end the mask slips as the scenes of cannibalism give way to Odysseus plying the Cyclops with drink:

> There's the Cyclops singing away on one side, my sailors howling away on the other, all round the cave. What a row.
> (lines 424–6)

A similar moment later in the play points to a comic technique where the illogical is played against the logical: 'I have no intention of deserting my men by beating a retreat' (line 478), announces Odysseus, who has succeeded in walking out of the cave but has not got round to suggesting that all the rest of the Greeks escape the same way,

> Though, of course, I could, me being outside the cave. But it wouldn't be fair for me to desert my companions – we came here together, after all – just to save my own skin.
> (lines 479–82)

Odysseus' ability to enter and exit from the cave at will must relate to the use of a side-entrance, less an apology for what would be an absurdity in real life, than a salute to a stage world and its conventions.

If Odysseus offers one kind of comic stolidity, he is matched by the ponderous villainy of the Cyclops whose ambitions stretch little further than his appetite. He becomes, drunk or sober, the obvious target for the satyrs, albeit a dangerous one. At one point the satyrs seem to play the 'master and servant' game, mocking him but trying to avoid being caught at it. And yet Euripides does provide for the Cyclops a speech of over thirty lines in which he proclaims the philosophy of self in language which amounts to a declaration of faith:

> The clever man's god is money. Everything else is wind and words . . . And all those who want to decorate man's life with morals, stuff 'em.
> (lines 316–17 and 338–40)

The moral debate may not reach a particularly exalted plane in *Cyclops*, but it is fundamental within the dramatic treatment. The attitudes which Polyphemus advocates may be those of the prime boor but they bear more than a passing resemblance to those of Paphlagon in Aristophanes' *Knights*, a play aimed directly at the politician Cleon.

Euripides' *Cyclops* has no direct political statement to make but the playing would allow for parody in a number of styles from Homeric recitation to contemporary oratory. Perhaps too the performance celebrated the sort of comic 'out takes' which occur in the most serious of rehearsal processes. A direct comparison between the concluding scene of *Cyclops* and the corresponding scene in *Hecuba* can be no more than marginal circumstantial evidence for their having formed part of the same submission. Most modern opinion, and notably, Richard Seaford in his definitive critical commentary (Oxford, Clarendon Press, 1984) prefer a date for *Cyclops* after 411 BC. Nonetheless, a comparison between the two blinding scenes is an interesting one. After Polymestor's children have been killed and he has been blinded by Hecuba's women in the tent, Polymestor returns to the stage. So does Polyphemus when his eye has been put out with the heated stake. Stage parody is often thought of in terms of exaggeration or over-emphasis – bad acting, in fact – but this is a limited and limiting view. To parody a performance it is necessary to suggest how to do it properly. The allocation of actors to playwrights makes it probable that the same actors played in all the plays of a playwright. That means the satyr play as well as the three tragedies.

The key to any echoes in performance lies less with the main characters than with the chorus. The antics and attitudes of the satyrs and of Silenus have a wonderful manic quality. Silenus will do or say anything to try and ensure his own security. The chorus, his sons, can only take so much of this and attempt to refute his accusations against Odysseus. They are creatures of instinct whether herding sheep, urging on Odysseus against Polyphemus or finding excuses not to give him a hand in dealing with the monster. What they really do is lead the audience into seeing the action through their eyes. It may well be that the difference between how a Polymestor or an Oedipus enter blind and how a Polyphemus does is chorus reaction. Fear and pity from the bystanders channel a similar response in the audience. Mockery makes an identical sequence of action comic.

Dramatic tone is not easy to gauge. In this example it relates both to occasion and to Dionysus' function as a god of regeneration as well as of catastrophe. Searching for a key to the satyr play in the introduction to his own *Trackers of Oxyrinchus* Tony Harrison points to the last line of *Cyclops* and the liberation of the satyrs from their servitude. 'The satyrs,' he states, 'are included in the wholeness of the tragic vision' (p. xi). And so they are. The arbitrariness of fate is a constant theme of most drama, not only classical. The new comedy of Menander had so little room to manoeuvre in the rigid social structure of his time that coincidence was elevated to godlike status. It has remained so ever since, especially in comedy, rivalled only by life itself.

The rapidity with which rank could be reduced through circumstance is a feature of any ancient society based on slavery. It is sometimes suggested that the Athenians simply failed to notice the underclass on which their privileged lives depended. If this is so, it is not reflected in their drama. *Hecuba* and *The Women of Troy* are shot through with the desolation of a queen reduced to a chattel. The fate of the Athenian soldiers in the stone quarries of Syracuse after the disastrous Sicilian expedition was what faced any prisoner-of-war. Personal servants were the fortunate ones, a standing achieved, it is said, by some of those Athenians who could recall Euripidean choruses and so become domestically negotiable.

High position to low, happiness to misery, the fickleness of Fate or *Tuche*, these are the stuff of a drama rooted in the Aristotelean principles of reversal and recognition. Conflict between the just and the unjust, the differences between the strong and the weak, find dramatic expression in a variety of ways reflecting rather than copying the real world. A tragic vision demanded a comic counterweight, so that what was hopeless for the individual should not create despair for the rest of the world.

The satyrs affirm the life-force in its most basic manifestation. Perhaps they do something more. Perhaps they propose the right not always to sympathise, not permanently to share the world's misery, because to do so is to lose sight of what survives in the face of what is dying. Prometheus' gift to mankind was 'wan hope'. Despair, to the medieval mind, was the sin that is not forgiven. We must beware of walking through the garden staring at the dead heads but ignoring the buds.

As a single philosophy this would be naive and as wanton as that of the Cyclops. As a fourth part of our existence, the first three of which are tragic, it may keep at bay a world whose persistent catalogue of misery flies in the face of any sense of human progress. Let the satyr play be art, humour, recreation and relaxation, going on leave from the trenches, the necessary survival kit for compassion. Let it serve as a justification for the theatre itself, whose impotence as a weapon Euripides had reason to regret. As a playwright he was adept enough at drawing attention to the wretchedness of the human condition in any and every area of life. That his plays still affect us in the theatre is as much a guarantee of that as the fact that his contemporaries tended to turn away their faces and disregard what he had to say. But through his one surviving satyr play a gleam of light does shine as a consolation for that bleakness of spirit. As Dionysus is less the obverse of Apollo than his darker twin, so the satyr play complements tragedy to make it whole. Dionysus offers the power of recuperation in the theatre as in life.

The line-numbering alongside the texts relates to the Greek original rather than the English translations.

J Michael Walton, 1991

Transliteration from Greek into English presents problems of consistency. The names of the playwrights are more familiar as Aeschylus, Sophocles and Menander than as Aischulos, Sophokles and Menandros. Otherwise direct transliteration has normally been adopted while allowing for previous translations in the series.

HECUBA

translated by Peter D Arnott

Characters

THE GHOST OF POLYDORUS, son of Hecuba
HECUBA, former Queen of Troy
POLYXENA, daughter of Hecuba
ODYSSEUS
TALTHYBIUS, Herald of the Greeks
SERVANT of Hecuba
AGAMEMNON, Commander-in-Chief of the Greek army
POLYMESTOR, King of Thrace
SONS of Polymestor (non-speaking)
CHORUS of Trojan women, prisoners of war, attendants, Greek and Thracian soldiers

Scene: The tents of the women prisoners in the Greek encampment near Troy.

Enter the ghost of POLYDORUS.

POLYDORUS.

Out of the dark door of the pit of death
I come, the shadow land where no god walks;
Polydorus, born the son of Hecuba
And Priam. When the danger came that Troy
Would fall before Greek spears, my father
Was afraid, and had me smuggled from the country
To his sworn friend Polymestor, King of Thrace,
Who farms the rich steppes of the Chersonese,
Iron-handed ruler of a race of horsemen.
He sent with me a secret store of gold   10
So his surviving sons might have no lack
Of livelihood, if Troy should ever fall.
I was the youngest of the sons of Priam
And so he sent me; I was still too young,
Too weak in arm to handle sword or shield.
So while our bastions still stood erect
And Trojan turrets were untouched by fire
And my brother Hector bore his spear in triumph
1 had fair treatment from my father's friend in Thrace
And flourished like a sapling – to my sorrow.   20
But then, when Hector breathed his last, Troy's last,
And the shrines my father built were tumbled down,
And he too, butchered by the bloody hands
Of Achilles' son at the altar of his gods,
He killed me for my gold, my father's friend,
Killed me, and threw my body in the sea
To have my gold to fill his treasury.
And so I drift between the sea and shore,
Borne by the waves on their returning courses,
Unmourned, unburied. Now I have left my body   30
To hover over my dear mother Hecuba.
This is the third day I have hovered here,
Three days that she has been away from Troy
To sorrow in this land of Chersonese.
The Greeks are bivouacked beside their ships
And time hangs heavy on the Thracian shore;

For as they cut the water with their oars
To sail for home, Achilles' ghost appeared
Above his tomb, and held the army back,
40   Demanding that Polyxena my sister
Be sacrificed, sweet honour to his grave.
And he will have her; he will not go unrewarded
By men who loved him. On this very day
My sister's destiny will lead her out to die,
And my mother will look upon the two dead bodies
Of her two children – mine and my poor sister's.
I shall appear, to find myself a grave,
Before a slave-girl wading in the shallows,
For I have moved the powers below to grant
50   That I be buried, and my mother find me;
And as I wished it, everything will come
To pass. Now I must walk out of the way
Of aged Hecuba. Look. She is coming out
Of Agamemnon's tent now, frightened by my ghost.
Oh mother, after courts of kings you see
This day of slavery – as miserable now
As you were happy then. Some god destroys you,
Exacting dues for past prosperity.

Exit POLYDORUS. *Enter* HECUBA, *attended*.

HECUBA.
Help the old woman out of doors, my children,
60   Lead me, Trojan women, hold me up; I was
Your queen once; now I am a slave like you.
Hold me, carry me, help me along.
Take my old arms and let me lean on you.
Your arms shall be my crutches
To lend motion to my feet,
One first, and then the other.
Lightning from heaven, dark of night,
Why am I so disturbed this night
70   By fears and phantoms? Lady Earth,
Mother of dreams that fly upon the dark,
I shrink from what I saw this night,
This nightmare that I had

About my son, who is safe in Thrace,
And Polyxena, the daughter that I love.
Gods of the dark earth, do not let him die!
He is the only anchor of my house, 80
He is alive among the snows of Thrace,
Ward of his father's friend.
Something dreadful is about to happen,
A new theme for our women's song of mourning.
My heart has never been so quick
With fear before, it will not rest.
Where is Helenus? He had
The power to prophesy; where is Cassandra?
They could read this dream for me.
I dreamt a fawn was lying on my lap 90
And then there came a wolf to savage it.
This is my fear:
Upon the summit of the tomb there stood
The phantom of Achilles,
Demanding one of the long suffering
Trojan women as a sacrifice.
Not my child! Not my child! I pray you,
You powers above us, keep her from this!

Enter the CHORUS.

CHORUS.

Hecuba, I come to you 100
Running from my masters' tents
Where lot assigned me as a slave
When I was driven from my city,
The spoils of war, the plunder
Of the Greeks who conquered Troy;
Not to make your sorrows lighter
But bowed with heavy news,
Grief's messenger for you, my lady.
They say the Greeks in convocation
Voted to offer up your daughter 110
As a sacrifice to Achilles.
Over his tomb he stood,
You remember, vivid in plated gold,

And held the searigged vessels
In harbour with his cry:
'Where are you going, men of Greece,
Leaving my tomb without honour?'
And then a wave of faction broke
And there were two minds running through
120 The armed assembly: some approved
The sacrifice, the rest did not.
Urging your interest was Agamemnon
Who has your daughter in his bed
To sleep with him, the prophetess;
And Theseus' sons, twin scions of Athens,
Though they spoke with different voices
Both met at one conclusion:
That Achilles' tomb must have its crown
Of fresh young blood. Cassandra's bed
130 They said should never rank before
The warrior Achilles.
Arguments flew and the issues were equal
Till the cunning honey-tongued prevaricator
Odysseus, who knows how to rouse a rabble,
Persuaded the army not to weigh
A living slave above a dead Greek hero,
And that none of the dead who stand beside
Persephone in the world below
140 Should call the Greeks ungrateful to their own
Who died for Greece, when they went away
And left the plains of Troy behind.
Odysseus is coming any moment
To drag your young one from your breast
And clutch of your aged arms.
Run to the temples, run to the altars,
Sit at Agamemnon's feet and pray for mercy;
Summon the gods in heaven above
And in the earth beneath.
150 If your tears cannot move them; if they take
Your wretched child away from you,
You will see her drop before the altar, and the blood

Will well between the necklace at her throat
And drop its dark stain on her.

HECUBA.

What do you say?
What sound, what sorrow?
Sad am I in sad old age,
Sad in bondage not to be endured
Or borne; who do I have
To save me now? What child? What country?   160
Priam is dead and gone, my sons are gone;
Which way am I to turn?
Where shall I run? What god, what power above
Will come to succour me?
Trojan women, bearers of evil,
Bearers of suffering and evil,
You have destroyed me, you have brought my death.
Life in the light is not worth living.
Take me, my unhappy feet,   170
Take the old woman back to her dwelling.
Daughter, child of wretched mother,
Leave the tent and come to me;
Hear what mother has to say,
My child, so you may know
What tale I have, what tale I have to tell
About your life.

Enter POLYXENA.

POLYXENA.

Mother; why are you calling, mother?
See, I am timid as a bird.
Why did you call me? Is there news?   180

HECUBA.

Oh, oh, my child . . .

POLYXENA.

A bad beginning. There is trouble . . .

HECUBA.

Oh, oh, your life . . .

POLYXENA.
Tell me, do not hide it any longer.
I am afraid, mother;
Afraid to see you cry.

HECUBA.
Oh child, your wretched mother's child . . .

POLYXENA.
Why are you saying this?

HECUBA.
The Greeks have had a meeting.
190   They want you for a sacrifice
Upon Achilles' tomb.

POLYXENA.
Mother, what is this dreadful thing
You are trying to say to me?
Tell me, tell me, mother.

HECUBA.
This is the story, and a curse is on it:
They say the Greeks have voted
That you must give your life.

POLYXENA.
Poor sufferer; poor broken one;
Poor luckless life, poor mother.
200   What pain, what agony,
What wild unspeakable revenge
Some god has raised against you.
No more shall I, your child, no more,
Wed young grief to your old grief
And share your bondage.
You will watch them take me from your hands
As if you were a beast and I your cub,
And you will weep to watch me die.
They will cut my throat, and send me
Into the dark below
210   To take my place among the mourning dead.
Mother, you were born to sorrow.
It is for you my sad tears flow.

My life, my ruin, my disgrace
I do not mourn. This is a lucky chance,
For me to die.

CHORUS.
I can see Odysseus hurrying here,
Hecuba, with the news for you.

Enter ODYSSEUS.

ODYSSEUS.
Madam, I think you know the army's mind
And how we voted. However, I'll repeat it.
The Greeks decreed that Polyxena your daughter   220
Should be sacrificed on the tall tomb of Achilles.
They have appointed us to act as escorts
And take the girl away. Achilles' son
Will supervise the sacrifice as priest.
You know what must be done. Please, no resistance.
Do not force us to resort to violence.
Acknowledge your weakness and your situation.
Be sensible. The facts are hard, but face them.

HECUBA.
So this must be my hour of reckoning.
No time for dry eyes, but for tears and mourning.   230
I did not die when it was time to die;
Zeus did not kill me then, but kept me living
To see more sorrow than the sorrows past.
If it is permitted for a slave to ask
Her master questions – not in bitterness
Or anger – you have spoken; it is well;
But you must listen when I ask of you.

ODYSSEUS.
Permission granted. Ask. I'm in no hurry.

HECUBA.
Do you remember when you came to Troy
To spy on us? You were in filthy rags,   240
And tears of blood were streaming down your face . . .

ODYSSEUS.
Of course. That day is graven on my heart.

HECUBA.
And Helen recognised you, and told me?

ODYSSEUS.
I ran a great risk, I remember well.

HECUBA.
You fell before me and abased yourself?

ODYSSEUS.
Yes. My fingers froze upon your robes.

HECUBA.
You were my slave then. What did you say to me?

ODYSSEUS.
I found a ready tongue to keep from dying.

HECUBA.
And I saved your life? I allowed you to escape?

ODYSSEUS.
250   Yes. That is why I am alive today.

HECUBA.
Then are you not ashamed of these contrivings,
When I used you as you admit I did,
To offer me no aid, but all the harm you can?
Oh, how I hate the sight of politicians,
Always taking, never giving; if your friends are hurt,
What does it mean to you? Your sole concern
Is saying something that will please the mob.
Tell me what policy they found in this,
To pass the vote of death against my daughter?
260   Did they have to offer human sacrifice
Upon the tomb, when custom asks for oxen?
If Achilles wants revenge on those
Who killed him, is it just to murder her?
She has never done him any harm.
He ought to ask for Helen's sacrifice.
She killed him. It is her fault he is here.
Or must it be the fairest of the prisoners?
Is this what you are after? What has this

To do with us? No, Helen is the beauty.
She has been found no less to blame than we are.   270
That is my case. I ask for simple justice.
But you also owe me a personal debt.
So hear me beg. You fell at my feet, you say,
And pressed my hand and touched my wrinkled cheek.
Now I am doing the same to you
And beg back the favour that I gave you then.
Have mercy! Don't tear my child from my arms,
Don't kill her. There are dead enough already.
In her I am happy, I forget my troubles.
I had so much; now she is my only comfort,   280
My nurse, my staff, my country and my guide.
The powerful should not abuse their power,
Or think that they will have good luck for ever.
I once was fortunate. Now look at me.
One day has taken all my joy in life.
I pray you by your beard, have pity on me,
Be merciful. Go back to the Greek army,
Persuade them it is tempting providence
To kill the women that you pitied once
And did not drag from sanctuary to die.   290
We have a law among us about killing.
It holds for free men and for slaves alike.
Your reputation will convince them, even if
Your heart's not in it; it's the speaker's name
That makes the difference, and not the speech.

CHORUS.
The man has not been born so hard of heart
That he could listen to you crying out
In agony, and not be moved by this.

ODYSSEUS.
Hecuba, I advise you to control yourself.
I am for you, not against you. Don't think otherwise.   300
Your person was my strength, and I'm prepared
To offer you protection. Yes, I mean it.
But I cannot go back on my public promise,

That when Troy fell our most distinguished soldier
Should have your daughter as a sacrifice.
It's detrimental to the public interest
For a hero who has volunteered his life
To have no more reward than a deserter.
Achilles has deserved our gratitude:

310 He died the best way any man could die – for Greece.
If we used a friend as long as he was living
And when he died had no more use for him,
Could we keep face? Suppose another war
Breaks out. Suppose we need another army.
What will men say? 'Shall we fight or run away?
See for yourself: no honour to the dead.'
I don't ask much of life while I'm alive.
Give me my daily needs, I'm satisfied.
But when I'm dead I want the world to see

320 My grave respected. That is lasting honour.
You say that you have suffered? Let me tell you,
We Greeks have mothers too, no bit less old
And grey and worn out by the world than you are,
And we have wives whose good men have been lost,
Their bodies buried in the soil of Troy.
So face the truth. As for us, if we do wrong
To honour the dead, then leave us to our folly.
But you barbarians go on refusing
To treat your friends as friends, dishonouring

330 The glorious dead; so Greece will be triumphant,
And you'll be done by as you did to others.

CHORUS.
This is the curse of slavery. It must bear
The ills and the abuses. Might is master.

HECUBA.
My daughter, all my pleading for your life
Has gone for nothing, words upon the wind.
If you have greater power than your mother
Go on, persuade him, try him with the tongues
Of nightingales, to make him spare your life.
Fall at Odysseus' feet and move his pity,

Win his heart; you have a claim, for he has children   340
Too, and he should pity your misfortune.

POLYXENA.

Odysseus, I can see you hide your hand
Under your cloak, and turn away your face
To stop me touching you. You need not worry.
I shall not ask my god to intervene.
I shall go with you, because I must
And because I want to die. If I did not
I should appear a weakling and a coward.
What have I to live for? Once my father was
King of all Trojans. So my life began,   350
And I was brought up with great expectations,
A bride for kings; and there was no small rivalry
To win my hand, and see whose home and hearth
I'd go to. I was first lady in the land;
I was the girl sought out by all men's eyes,
Peer of the gods, except that I must die.
Now I am a slave. The very name
Makes me in love with death, it is so strange.
It might well be my lot to fall among
Hard-hearted masters, and the man who buys me,   360
Sister of Helen and so many brothers,
Will make me kitchen-servant in his home,
Set me to sweep the house, and stand beside
The loom, and fill my day with bitterness.
Perhaps some purchased slave will come to stain
My bed, once counted worthy of a king.
It shall not be. My eyes bid their farewell
To light and freedom. Death shall have my body.
Take me, Odysseus, and do what you want.
I have no hope, no shadow of a hope   370
That better days will ever come again.
Mother, do not say anything to interfere
Or try to stop me. Share in my desire
To die before dishonour comes, and shame.
When you have never known the taste of sorrow,
You may bear it, but the yoke will gall your neck.
And I would be far happier to die
Than live; for life hangs heavy without honour.

CHORUS.
>Breeding tells. It sets its stamp on men
380 >And marks them out, bestowing on the worthy
>A greater title to nobility.

HECUBA.
>Your words are good, my daughter; but the good
>Is mixed with sorrow. If Achilles must
>Receive his due reward, and you avoid
>Reproach, Odysseus, do not kill my daughter.
>Take me away to where his pyre is laid,
>Strike, have no mercy; Paris was my son,
>And it was Paris' arrow killed Achilles.

ODYSSEUS.
>It was not your death that Achilles' ghost
390 >Demanded of the Greeks, old queen, but hers.

HECUBA.
>Then sacrifice me by my daughter's side,
>And twice the blood will flow in offerings
>For earth and for the dead man who demands it.

ODYSSEUS.
>One girl must die. No more. We must not add
>A second death. I wish this one were spared us.

HECUBA.
>But I must die beside my child! I must!

ODYSSEUS.
>Must? Since when have you been giving orders?

HECUBA.
>I shall cling to her like ivy to the oak.

ODYSSEUS.
>Not if you listen to what is good for you.

HECUBA.
400 >I'll never give her up, so do not think it!

ODYSSEUS.
>And I'll not go away from here without her.

POLYXENA.
>Mother, do as I say. Odysseus, be patient

With my mother in her anger. She has cause.
Poor mother, do not try to fight your masters.
Do you want to be thrown in the dirt, be tossed aside
By young arms, drag your poor old bones away
Humiliated? That is what will happen.
No. Not you. It is unworthy of you.
My darling mother, let me hold the hand
I love best in the world, lay your cheek to mine.   410
Bright disk of the sun, I look on you now
For the last time, never again.
Hear the last words I shall ever say.
I am going, mother. Going below.

HECUBA.
And I to live, my child, and be a slave.

POLYXENA.
Robbed of my marriage, cheated of my rights . . .

HECUBA.
Tears are your portion, daughter, mine is sorrow . . .

POLYXENA.
I shall lie there in death, away from you . . .

HECUBA.
What shall I do? How shall I end my days?

POLYXENA.
The daughter of a free man dies a slave . . .   420

HECUBA.
Fifty children, all of them gone . . .

POLYXENA.
What message to Hector and your old husband?

HECUBA.
Say I suffer as no one ever has before.

POLYXENA.
Breast where I drew life and smiled . . .

HECUBA.
Daughter dead before your time . . .

POLYXENA.
Farewell, mother. Farewell to Cassandra.

HECUBA.

Others fare well, but your mother never.

POLYXENA.

And brother Polydorus with the Thracian horsemen.

HECUBA.

If he lives. I doubt it. All my hopes are blighted.

POLYXENA.

430   He lives. He'll close your eyes when you are dead.

HECUBA.

But I have died before my death in sorrow.

POLYXENA.

Take me, Odysseus. Cover up my face.
Before I feel the knife my mother's grief
Has rent my heart, and I rend hers with mourning.
O light of day – I still may speak your name,
But you are mine for but that little time
In which I pass between the sword and flames.

Exeunt ODYSSEUS *and* POLYXENA.

HECUBA.

Oh, I am faint, I cannot stand.
Touch your mother, child; where is your hand?
440   Here; do not leave me childless. Oh, my friends,
This is the end. If Helen were here now,
The Spartan woman, sister of twin gods,
Whose smiles have fouled the glory that was Troy!

CHORUS.

O wind upon the waters,
That sends the vessels scudding
Across the swirling sea,
Where will you bear me now?
And whose house shall I enter
As a chattel and a slave?
450   To some Dorian harbour town,
Or Phthia, where Apidanus,
The father of fair rivers, brings
His bounty to the fields?

Or will the driving oarstroke
Transport me to the islands
To house my heavy head,
Where first the palm tree grew
And holiness of laurel
Keeping green the name of Leto   460
Who was hard delivered there?
And when the girls of Delos hymn
The crown and bow of Artemis,
Shall I be at their side?

Or shall I take up my abode
Where Pallas dwells, in chariot and glory,
To ply and pattern at the loom,
Linking a skein of horses
And garlands, gay devices   470
As ornament for her saffron robe,
Or the family of Titans
That were laid to rest by Zeus
With a fork of heaven's fire?

Cry for the desolation of
My children and my fathers, for the smoke
And darkness fallen on the land.
Cry for the waste and havoc,
The might of Greece that conquered.
My name shall be slave in a foreign land;   480
I shall leave the halls of Asia
And in Europe make my home,
In the waiting room of death.

Enter TALTHYBIUS.

TALTHYBIUS.
  Women of Troy, where may I find
  Hecuba, who used to be your queen?

CHORUS.
  You are standing next to her, Talthybius.
  There. Lying on the ground, wrapped in her robes.

TALTHYBIUS.
  What can I say? Is there a seeing god,

Or have we all deceived ourselves with lies,
490   Imagining that there are powers above us?
Is it blind chance that oversees our lives?
Was this not once the queen of golden Troy,
Wife of Priam the magnificent?
Now war has razed her city; there she lies
Prostrate, a slave, her youth and children gone,
In misery, her hair bedraggled in the dust.
I am an old man, but I'd pray to die
Before such degradation fell upon me.
Lady of sorrows, rise; lift up your body
500   From off the ground, and raise your snow-white head.

HECUBA.
Who is it will not let my body lie?
Who are you? Why do you disturb my grief?

TALTHYBIUS.
Talthybius, madam, herald of the Greeks.
Agamemnon ordered me to come.

HECUBA.
Oh, you are welcome! Have the Greeks decided
To sacrifice me too? Say yes, I'll love you for it.
Hurry, let's waste no time, good herald, take me.

TALTHYBIUS.
No, madam. I have come to summon you
To bury your daughter. This is the command
510   Laid on me by our generals and the army.

HECUBA.
What are you saying? You have not brought
News of my death, but only of my sorrow?
Child, you are dead, gone from your mother.
In you I am now childless. Weep for Hecuba!
How did you kill her? Was it with respect,
Or did you come like murderers to kill
The one you hate? Though it be bitter, tell me.

TALTHYBIUS.
You bid me take a double load of tears
In pity for your daughter. When I tell her death

I shall weep as at the graveside when she died.   520
The whole Greek army was assembled there
Around the tomb to watch her sacrificed.
Achilles' son took Polyxena by the hand
And set her on the tomb-mound. I was near her,
And there were youths selected from the Greeks
Behind us, who would hold your daughter still
If she showed resistance. Achilles' son
Lifted a cup full to its golden brim
To pour to his dead father. Then he signalled me
To call for silence in the ranks assembled.   530
I stepped into the midst of them and cried
'Greeks, be silent; let no man here present
Utter a word.' A deep hush fell upon them.
He spoke. 'O son of Peleus, my father,
Receive from my hand this propitious draught
To raise the dead; come, rise and drink dark blood
Fresh from a virgin that we offer you,
The army and myself. Look kindly on us
And let us loose the cables from our ships
And sail from Troy. Grant us a happy voyage   540
And let us see our fatherland again.'
So he spoke. The army joined in prayer.
Then he drew the two-edged golden sword
Out of its scabbard, and nodded to
The chosen youths to hold your daughter down.
But when she heard the order she addressed them:
'Men of Greece, destroyers of my city,
I am a willing victim. Do not touch me.
I yield my throat to you with all good will.
For god's love, leave me free when you despatch me   550
And let me die free. I should be ashamed
For the dead to call me slave. I am a princess.'
There was a ripple of applause, and Agamemnon
Ordered the youths to let the maiden go.
They dropped their hands at once upon his word;
When Agamemnon orders, no one disobeys.
When she heard their master give the word
She seized her dress and ripped it from the clasp

That pinned it on her shoulder to the navel
560   Uncovering her lovely marble breasts.
And then she knelt down on the ground, and spoke
As moving words as I have ever heard:
'Here is my breast, young man, if this is where
You wish to strike. But if it is
My neck you want, cut here. My throat is ready.'
Half willing, half unwilling out of pity
He cut with sword the passage of her breath
And fountains flowed. But even as she died
Her last thought was to fall with decency
570   Hiding what should be hidden from men's eyes.
When breath had left the rent the sword had made
The Greeks set to work, every man to his task.
Some gathered armfuls of leaves, and strewed them
Over her body; others went for logs
To heap the pyre. If anybody came
With empty hands, his busy mates abused him:
'Why are you standing idle? Go and bring
A robe or some adornment for the lady.
Find her an offering. She had great heart,
580   As brave as the best.' That is all I have to tell
Of your dead daughter. Of all women I have seen
You are most blessed in your children, and most cursed.

CHORUS.

For Priam and his sons and for my city
The bitter cup runs over. It is god's decree.

HECUBA.

Child, which sorrow shall I look to first?
I have so many. When I grasp at one
Another beckons me, some newer grief
Distracts me and comes treading on its heels.
And now I cannot wipe your fate from mind
590   To check my tears; but I shall weep the less
Through being told of your nobility.
Strange, if poor land bears good harvest
When blessed by gods with growing weather

While good land lacking its necessities
Yields poor crops; but in our human lot
The bad are bad and never change their natures;
The good are always good and under stress
Retain their virtue, upright to the end.
What makes the difference? Is it in the parents
Or in the rearing? To be well brought up   600
Is to be schooled in virtue; learn your lesson well
And you will know vice too, by virtue's measure.
But these are flights at random. Go back to the Greeks
And make this proclamation. Tell them nobody
Must lay hands on my daughter. Keep the crowd
Away from her. In such a countless muster
Licence is king, and riot in the fleet
Spreads worse than forest fire. It is a crime then
To do no crime.

Exit TALTHYBIUS.

                 Old servant, take your pitcher,
Fill it with sea water, bring it back to me,   610
So I may bathe my daughter at the last,
Bride but no bride, virgin but no virgin,
And lay her out . . . as she deserves? I cannot;
Yet as I may . . . how can I do enough?
Go gather things among the captive women
Who live beside me in these tents, my neighbours,
To dress her; see if they have something stolen
Out of their homes, to cheat their new masters.

Exit an ATTENDANT.

O glory of my house; once blessed palace,
Almighty Priam, happy in your sons,   620
And I, who was the mother of your children.
Look at us: come to nothing, stripped of all
Our former pride. Oh, how we preen ourselves:
One man glories in the riches of his palace,
Another in the popular applause.
These things are nothing, empty self-delusion
And idle words. The greatest happiness
Is living safe from one day to the next.

Exit HECUBA.

CHORUS.

My ruin and disaster
630 Were born upon that day
When out of Ida's forest
Paris felled himself a tree
To take him voyaging across the surge
Of waters into Helen's bed,
Of all the women that the sun
Shines golden on, the loveliest.

Now I am bound with hardship
Made harder by constraint,
For out of one man's folly
640 Came the wasting of the land
And havoc wrought by others. So the strife
Was ended that the shepherd sought
To judge between the trinity
Of blessed ones, the goddesses,

With blood and war and ruin of my house.
In her house by fair Eurotas
Sits a Spartan woman crying,
And a mother who is tearing
Her grey hair with her hands
650 And rends her face in mourning
Because her sons are dead.

Enter SERVANTS *with the body of* POLYDORUS *covered.*

SERVANT.

Ladies, where is Hecuba, the queen of sorrows
Who in the number of her griefs surpasses
660 All man and womankind, and yields the crown to none?

CHORUS.

Why do you cry? What sad tale is it now?
Your mouth is full of them. They never rest.

SERVANT.

This grief's for Hecuba. When trouble comes
It's difficult to keep a silent tongue.

CHORUS.
Look. She is coming now, outside her tent.
This is the right time. Talk to her.

Enter HECUBA.

SERVANT.
My queen, more wretched than I can say,
Death has come to take you open-eyed
The way of Priam, of your sons and Troy.

HECUBA.
This is no news. I know the worst already.   670
Why have you brought Polyxena's body?
What is it doing here? They told me
The Greeks were busy building her a grave.

SERVANT.
She knows nothing. She weeps for Polyxena still;
This grief is new. She cannot grasp it yet.

HECUBA.
No! Never tell me you bring Cassandra,
My godly child, the prophetess?

SERVANT.
Cries for the living, no tears for the dead.
Uncover the body, look upon its face:
Is this as you expected it would be?   680

HECUBA (*uncovering the body*).
This is my son Polydorus. He is dead.
But the Thracian was keeping him safe in his palace . . .
My life has ended here. There is no Hecuba.
O my child,
Here in the madness of my grief
I cry for you; I know at last
The vengeance and the suffering.

SERVANT.
Now do you see? This was his fate.

HECUBA.
I see, but cannot believe my eyes;

690   Blow upon blow, one follows the other . . .
       No day shall see the end of my tears;
       Now I shall weep for all eternity.

CHORUS.
       This is a dreadful thing that they have done to us.

HECUBA.
       Child, child of ill-starred mother,
       How are you dead? What fortune struck you down?
       Who was the man that killed you?

SERVANT.
       I do not know. I found him on the shore.

HECUBA.
       Murdered, butchered by the spear
700   And cast out on the beach?

SERVANT.
       The waves had carried him and let him lie.

HECUBA.
       And now, oh now, my nightmare has a meaning;
       It has come home to me, that thing
       That flew to haunt me on the night,
       The vision that I saw of you,
       My child, who can no longer see the sun.

CHORUS.
       Who killed him? Can you read that in your dream?

HECUBA.
710   It was my friend, my friend, the Thracian horseman
       With whom his aged father had him hidden.

CHORUS.
       What do you mean? He killed him for his gold?

HECUBA.
       A deed without a name, without example,
       Gross and blasphemous; have friends no rights?
       You devil, how you mangled him
       And hacked him with your sword;
720   There was no pity in you, none.

CHORUS.

>A god has laid his heavy hand upon you
>And greatest suffering that man can know.
>But here is our master Agamemnon.
>It is time for us to hold our tongues.

Enter AGAMEMNON.

AGAMEMNON.

>Hecuba, why have you not yet come
>To lay your daughter in her tomb? Talthybius
>Reported that you did not want the Greeks to touch her,
>So we left her where she was, and undisturbed.
>I wondered why you took so long to come   730
>And came to fetch you. All has been well seen to
>There – as well as anything can be.
>But who is this I see beside the tent?
>The body of a Trojan: not a Greek,
>I know that by the clothes that he has on.

HECUBA (*aside*).

>Oh, wretched – there's a name for both of us –
>Hecuba, what shall I do? Fall at the feet
>Of Agamemnon here, or bear my grief in silence?

AGAMEMNON.

>Why do you turn your back on me and weep?
>What has happened here? Who is this man?   740

HECUBA (*aside*).

>But if he treats me as his enemy, his slave
>And spurns me, I'll have added to my troubles.

AGAMEMNON.

>I have no second sight. I cannot tell
>The passage of your thought unless you speak.

HECUBA (*aside*).

>Or am I too much reckoning his mind
>To be an enemy's when he is not?

AGAMEMNON.

>If you do not want to tell me what has happened
>That suits us both. I do not want to hear.

HECUBA (*aside*).

    I am not able to avenge my children

750   Without his help. Why stand here wondering?

    Win or lose, I have to do my best.

    Agamemnon, I beseech you by your knees

    And by your beard, and by your blest right hand –

AGAMEMNON.

    What is it that you want? To live your life

    In freedom? That can easily be granted.

HECUBA.

    No! To take vengeance on my enemies

    Then be a slave, and gladly, till I die.

AGAMEMNON.

    What assistance do you want from me?

HECUBA.

    Not what you think, my lord.

760   You see this body, still wet with my tears?

AGAMEMNON.

    Yes. But the rest is still a mystery.

HECUBA.

    This is the child I carried in my womb.

AGAMEMNON.

    One of your sons? You have my sympathy.

HECUBA.

    And Priam's. But he did not die at Troy.

AGAMEMNON.

    You had another son, as well as those?

HECUBA.

    The one you see. If I had only known!

AGAMEMNON.

    Where was he, when the city was destroyed?

HECUBA.

    His father feared for his life, and sent him off –

AGAMEMNON.

    Away from his brothers? Where did he go?

HECUBA.
> Here. This country. Where we found him dead. 770

AGAMEMNON.
> You mean to the king here? Polymestor?

HECUBA.
> He carried gold with him. O cruel gold!

AGAMEMNON.
> How was he murdered? By what man's hand?

HECUBA.
> Who else? It was our Thracian friend who killed him.

AGAMEMNON.
> No doubt because he coveted his gold.

HECUBA.
> As soon as he discovered Troy had fallen.

AGAMEMNON.
> Where was he found? Who brought you his body?

HECUBA.
> My servant. She discovered him on the beach.

AGAMEMNON.
> Looking for him, or by accident?

HECUBA.
> Fetching water for Polyxena. 780

AGAMEMNON.
> Your friend had killed him, then and cast him off.

HECUBA.
> See these gashes; and the marks made by the sea.

AGAMEMNON.
> Poor lady, will your hardships never end?

HECUBA.
> I have known the sum of sorrow. I am nothing now.

AGAMEMNON.
> Was ever woman so unfortunate?

HECUBA.
> None, unless Misfortune came in person.

Now listen why I sit in supplication
Here at your feet. If you think I have deserved this
Then I have no complaints. But if not, help me:
790 Punish that devil who called himself my friend
And did this monstrous, blasphemous thing
Without fear for the living or the dead.
He has eaten at my board a hundred times,
Stood first among the number of my friends:
All I was bound to give, and more, I gave him.
Yet he killed my son; and if that were not enough,
Thought burial too good for him, and threw him in the sea.
I am a slave. A poor thing is a slave,
But strong the gods, and strong the law which gives
800 The gods their being: so we believe in them
And live our lives dividing right from wrong.
So if your judgement disallows this law,
If men can lie and steal and not be punished
And violate the high commands of heaven,
There is no justice left upon this earth:
Abominate these things and show me mercy.
Have pity on me; stand off, look at me
As at a picture, see my sufferings.
I was a queen once; now I am your slave.
810 Proud mother once, and now a lone old woman,
Homeless, forlorn, of all mankind most wretched.
You turn away? Oh, poor fool that I am,
I see I can do nothing. Fool indeed:
Why do we study other sciences,
We mortals, and pursue them with such pains
Instead of spending labour mastering
Persuasion, which alone is lord of men?
And hiring teachers in that art, so man
Might set his wish to words and move his hearers?
820 For there's our only hope of victory.
The children that I had are mine no more,
I end my days in shame, a prisoner,
And stand here looking at my city burn.
I know it's hollow talk for me to urge
The claims of love, and yet it shall be spoken.

You have my daughter as your bedfellow,
The prophetess the Trojans call Cassandra.
How will you mark those nights of joy, my lord?
What favour shall she have, and I from her,
For those delectable embracings in your bed?   830
For in the darkness when the lights are out
Come lovers' charms to warm the hearts of men.
So listen to me now. You see this dead boy here?
Help him, and you help one who is your kin.
But there's still one thing lacking to my story.
If some device of god, some man's invention
Could give my arms, hands, hair, the going of
My feet, a tongue and teach them how to speak,
Till all my body was one voice, to weep
Before you and to fill your ears with pleading!   840
My lord and master, shining light of Greece,
Do as I ask; lend your avenging hand
To this old woman. She is nothing . . . still,
Great spirits show themselves in serving justice
And paying evil back as it deserves.

CHORUS.
Life is full of strange concurrences
And men make partners from necessity.
Those we hated most become our friends,
Our once loved friends become our enemies.

AGAMEMNON.
You, Hecuba, your son, your misery,   850
Your pleading hands, all call upon my pity.
In the name of justice and the gods, I wish
I could punish your perjuring friend for you.
If there were some way you could have your wish
Without the army thinking I had worked
The death of Polymestor for Cassandra's sake!
That's the dilemma I am caught in now.
The army calls the murderer their friend,
His victim their enemy. If he's a friend of mine
That is my business, no concern of theirs.   860
You must think of this. I'm ready and anxious

To help; but if it means I must lose face
With the Greeks, I must tread more cautiously.

HECUBA.

No man upon this earth is truly free.
He's a slave to his purse-strings, a slave to fortune,
Or public opinion or the force of law
Keep him from living according to his nature.
If you worry so much what people will say
I'll free you from this apprehension.

870   If I can find some way to hurt this murderer,
Share the knowledge only, not the deed;
And if the Greeks riot, or try to rescue
Our Thracian friend when there comes to him
What shall come, stop them. Do not say it is for me.
Don't worry. I shall see to all the rest.

AGAMEMNON.

Yes, but how? Can a woman of your age
Handle a sword, and kill this savage?
Or poison him? What help can you rely on?
Who'll stand beside you? Where will you find friends?

HECUBA.

880   In these tents, a secret army – Trojan women!

AGAMEMNON.

You mean the prisoners? The spoils of war?

HECUBA.

With them to help me I shall be revenged.

AGAMEMNON.

How can women have the strength of men?

HECUBA.

There's strength in numbers. And we have surprise.

AGAMEMNON.

In numbers, yes . . . but all the same, these women –

HECUBA.

Why not? Who was it killed Aegyptus' sons
And emptied Lemnos of its men? The women!
So be it. No more talk. Do this for me:

Let this woman have safe conduct through the lines.
Go to my Thracian friend, and say to him   890
'Hecuba, who was once Queen of Troy
Summons you and your sons – for your advantage
As well as hers. Your sons must hear her message
As well as you.'

Exit SERVANT.

      Agamemnon, do not let them
Bury my new dead daughter for a while.
She shall burn with her brother. Let me mourn them both,
And let the earth enfold them side by side.

AGAMEMNON.
So be it, then. If the army had it in its power
To sail, I could never have granted you this favour.
But as god gives us no fair wind   900
We have to wait upon good sailing weather.
May all go well! This is the rule
For nations and individuals alike;
Wrong suffers wrong, and the righteous prosper.

Exit AGAMEMNON. *The body is covered.*

CHORUS.
Mother Troy, no longer shall your name
Be spoken of among unravished cities.
Now you are veiled; a cloud of Greeks
Hangs on you, armed for plunder.
And your coronet of towers   910
Is docked now; palls of smoke
Lie black on you, defiling.
I shall never tread you more.

It was midnight when my ruin came,
When sleep succeeds the banquet, and comes welcome
Over the eyes. The songs were stilled,
And chorals at the altar,
And my lord hung up his spear   920
To lay him down to sleep,
Keeping no watch for sailors
To come thronging into Troy.

I was putting up my hair
In bands, to bind it tight,
Before my gilded mirror's
Bright unfathomable gaze,
Ready to sink into bed and sleep.
And then there was a clamour through the streets
930   And shouting in the city: 'Sons of Greece,
When is the day? When will you take
The citadel of Troy, and go
Back to your homes again?'

Then I fled my friendly bed
Dressed like a Doric girl
In shift alone, and prayed to
Holy Artemis in vain.
And I have seen my husband dead, and go
Against my will across the wide salt sea.
I looked back at my city, when the ship
940   Started for home, and sundered me
From Troy that was my land, and fell
Faint on the deck from grief,

And laid my curse upon
The sister of the Twin Gods, Helen,
And Paris the shepherd, god's judgement on Ida.
For the marriage that was none,
But a vengeance to destroy us
Has lost me home and country.
950   Waters, never bear her home
Or let her see her land again.

Enter POLYMESTOR *with his two small sons.*

POLYMESTOR.
O Priam whom I loved above all others,
And Hecuba! I weep to see your city
And for your daughter, newly taken from you.
Nothing is safe. A good name may be lost;
Things may go well today and not tomorrow.
The gods are always shuffling our affairs,
Creating chaos, so we worship them,

Through fear of the unknown. Why count your losses?   960
You never forge ahead of trouble. Are you
Angry with me for not coming? Wait
A moment; I was away when you arrived,
In the centre of my country. I had just returned.
Your servant caught me at the very moment
I was about to leave my house and find you.
I listened to her tale, and here I am.

HECUBA.

I am ashamed to look you in the face,
Polymestor, in the midst of my misfortunes.
I feel such shame that anyone who saw me   970
In happier days should see me now, distressed.
I could not lift my eyes to look at you.
But do not think that I am angry with you,
Polymestor; I make custom my excuse,
That women drop their eyes in menfolk's presence.

POLYMESTOR.

I understand. What was it that you wanted?
Why did you send to the palace for me?

HECUBA.

I have a secret for your ears, and for
Your children's too. Instruct your bodyguards
To leave the tent and keep their distance.   980

POLYMESTOR.

Dismiss. This place is empty, we are safe.
You are my friend; but the Greeks and I
Are friendly too. But come now: you must tell me
How a man who has had better luck
Can help friends in distress. I am at your service.

HECUBA

Begin by telling me about my son.
You took him from our hands into your home.
Is he alive? The other things can wait.

POLYMESTOR.

Of course. You're still in luck where he's concerned.

HECUBA.

Well said, dear friend, and spoken like yourself.   990

POLYMESTOR.
  What else is it you want to ask of me?

HECUBA.
  Does he remember who his mother is?

POLYMESTOR.
  Enough to try to cross the lines to see you.

HECUBA.
  And the gold he brought from Troy? Is that still safe?

POLYMESTOR.
  Safe, under lock and key in my palace.

HECUBA.
  Let it stay so. Covet not your neighbour's goods.

POLYMESTOR.
  I hope my own will give me joy enough.

HECUBA.
  Can you guess what I want to tell you and your children?

POLYMESTOR.
  How can I guess? Speak out, and let me hear.

HECUBA.
1000   Friend, dear as you are dear to me, there is –

POLYMESTOR.
  There's what? What must we know, my sons and I?

HECUBA.
  An ancient treasure of the house of Priam.

POLYMESTOR.
  You want to send this message to your son?

HECUBA.
  Yes, through you; I know you can be trusted.

POLYMESTOR.
  But why do my children have to come along?

HECUBA.
  You might be killed. It's better they should know.

POLYMESTOR.
A good idea. So much the wiser you.

HECUBA.
You know where Athene's temple stands in Troy?

POLYMESTOR.
Is that where the gold is? Did you leave a mark?

HECUBA.
Yes. A black stone sticking from the ground.   1010

POLYMESTOR.
Is there anything else I need to know?

HECUBA.
I brought away some money. Will you hold it?

POLYMESTOR.
Where do you keep it? Hidden in your clothes?

HECUBA.
Under a heap of plunder in my tent.

POLYMESTOR.
Here? With the Greek ships beached all round you?

HECUBA.
Only the women prisoners use these tents.

POLYMESTOR.
Is it safe to go in? There are no men here?

HECUBA.
There are no Greeks inside. No one but women.
No, come inside my tent. The Greeks are anxious
To sail for home. They have had enough of Troy.   1020
You can do all you have to do, and take
Your children back to where you left my son.

HECUBA, POLYMESTOR *and the children go inside the
tent.*

CHORUS.
You go without fear, but the judgement waits:
Like a drowning man out of sight of land
You will lose your being and your heart's desire.
When justice and the gods go hand in hand

1030   They ask a penalty, and it is death.
          You will be cheated in your road,
          Which leads you to the dark world, dead,
          Leaving your life in hands not made for war.

POLYMESTOR (*within*).
          They have blinded me! I cannot see!

CHORUS.
          Listen, my friends! Do you hear him scream?

POLYMESTOR.
          And now I cry for you, my slaughtered sons!

CHORUS.
          Friends, there has been strange work done inside.

POLYMESTOR.
          You'll not escape! You'll never slip away!
1040   I'll break out of the confines of this tent . . .

CHORUS.
          Listen how he hammers with his hands!
          This is the crisis and the summons: shall we run
          To Hecuba, and lend our strength to theirs?

HECUBA *re-enters*.

HECUBA.
          Hammer at the doors, and smash them down!
          You'll never put the light back in those eyes
          Or see your sons alive again. I killed them!

CHORUS.
          Is it true, my lady? Have you mastered him?
          Is he your victim now, this friend from Thrace?

HECUBA.
          You will see yourselves: he is coming out,
1050   Tripping, stumbling, blind in eyes and feet;
          And the bodies of his sons: I killed them both
          With my brave Trojan women. He has paid
          The debt he owed me. Watch him, here he comes.
          I must avoid him, stand out of his way:
          He is mad, this Thracian lion, mad and dangerous.

          Enter POLYMESTOR, *blind*.

POLYMESTOR.
    Where shall I go? Where shall I stand?
    Where shall I run for shelter?
    I go upon my hands and knees,
    Crawling like an animal.
    Shall I turn to left or right   1060
    To find them, get my hands on them,
    These women, Trojans, murderers?
    Oh, you womenfolk of Troy,
    My curse is on you: where have you run
    To hide yourselves away?
    Sun, lend me your light;
    Heal, heal my sightless eyes,
    For they are running blood, and blind.
    Quiet! I hear the stealthy step
    Of women; where can I run   1070
    To fall upon them, crush them in my arms,
    Eat them as a wolf devours his prey,
    Rend them, tear them and destroy them
    As they did me? But, oh,
    Where am I going, leaving my sons
    To be torn asunder by these fiends from hell,
    To be cast out on the mountainside
    And given to the dogs to eat?
    Where can I go or stand or turn,
    Girding up my robe about me   1080
    Like a ship before the wind,
    Falling on this plague of women
    So they will not touch my sons!

CHORUS.
    Poor man, some god has laid his hand upon you
    To work your downfall, and returned to you
    Evil for evil as you deserved.

POLYMESTOR.
    Thracians, take your spears in hand,
    Arm and mount, and come to me,
    All who serve the God of War!   1090
    Greeks, to you and your kings

I call aloud and cry:
Come, for gods' love come to me!
Do you hear? Will no man help?
Why do you wait? The women have destroyed me,
The women, the prisoners; come and see
This dreadful thing that they have done,
This bloody work, this outrage!
Where can I turn? Where can I go?

1100   Shall I take wing, and fly
Into the heights of heaven
Where Sirius and Orion dwell
And shoot fire from their eyes?
Or down to that dark ferryman
Who rows the dead to their final home?

CHORUS.
When troubles have grown beyond endurance
It is no crime to kill yourself.

Enter AGAMEMNON *with soldiers.*

AGAMEMNON.
I came when I heard you scream. The child

1110   Of the high hills, Echo, did not hush her voice
But clamoured through the army. If we did not know
That Troy had fallen and the war was over
This noise would have alarmed us not a little.

POLYMESTOR.
Agamemnon, my friend! I know you by your voice:
Do you see what they have done to me?

AGAMEMNON.
Polymestor! Who did this to you?
Who gave you these bleeding holes for eyes,
And murdered your children? How he must
Have hated them and you, to do this thing.

POLYMESTOR.

1120   It was Hecuba and the women prisoners
Who killed me – no, they did far worse than kill me!

AGAMEMNON.
   What! Hecuba, is he telling the truth?
   Did you dare to do this monstrous thing?

POLYMESTOR.
   What, is she somewhere near me now?
   Show her to me, tell me where she is!
   I want to hug her and tear her to pieces!

AGAMEMNON.
   What are you doing?

POLYMESTOR.
             For the love of god
   Let me go; my hands are itching for her.

AGAMEMNON.
   Keep back, you brute, control yourself.
   Tell me why you have been hurt like this   1130
   So I can hear both sides and judge between you.

POLYMESTOR.
   Gladly. There was a boy, Polydorus,
   Hecuba's and Priam's youngest son.
   His father sent him to my home for safety,
   Fearing in his heart that Troy would fall.
   I killed that boy, and I'll tell you why:
   I did right, and I knew what I was doing.
   I feared if this boy lived to fight again
   He might build a new Troy, and reunite its people;
   And if the Greeks knew a young Priam was alive   1140
   They might send another army into Asia
   And march across my country, burning, raping,
   Killing; it would not be healthy then
   To be Troy's neighbour. We've been hurt enough in
                         this war.
   When Hecuba knew her son was dead
   She lured me with a tale of buried treasure,
   Gold belonging to the sons of Priam
   In Troy. She brought me to her tent alone
   With my children, so that no one else should hear it.

1150   I sat down in the middle of her bed.
       On my right the Trojan women clustered round me
       And on my left, pretending to be friendly,
       They sat there and admired my Thracian clothes,
       Feasting their eyes on these robes I wear.
       Others inspected my Thracian lance
       And took my double spear away from me.
       All who were mothers there admired my children,
       And danced them on their knees, and took them from
       Their father's side, and passed them down the line.
1160   And then what happened! All the fine talk ended.
       They whipped out swords from underneath their robes
       And stabbed my sons, while others rounded on me
       And helped their friends by hanging to my arms
       And legs. I struggled to get to my sons,
       But when I tried to lift my head
       They held me by the hair. As for using my arms,
       What strength had I against a mob of women?
       Then came the end, the crowning horror,
       A hideous thing: they took their brooches
1170   And stabbed my eyes – I had no way to stop them –
       Till they were blood. And then they ran away
       And scattered through the tents. I leaped up after them
       Baying on these murderous bitches' heels
       And driving them from cover, flailing out
       And striking at them. This I suffered, Agamemnon,
       For working in your interest and killing
       Your enemy. To cut a long tale short,
       Whoever in the past has cursed at women,
       Or curses now, or ever in the future,
1180   I'll say it for him in a few short words:
       Earth and water never spawned their like.
       You only have to meet with them to know.
   CHORUS.
       You go too far. You must not let your troubles
       Make you judge all women harshly.
       Some are born bad. There are others
       Hated by the world unjustly.

HECUBA.

Agamemnon, when we look at men we should not
Let their words speak louder than their deeds.
If a man's life has been honest, then his words should be;
And if he lives a lie, his words are rotten.   1190
Foul deeds must not be covered in fine phrases.
There are men who have this at their fingers' ends,
But they are not so clever, in the last resort:
Their sins will find them out. There can be no escape.
That for my prologue. This is meant for you.

And now it is my turn to answer him.
Yes, you, who say you killed my son to spare
Greece double labour, and for Agamemnon.
You liar! First of all, there's no love lost
Between the Greeks and the barbarians,   1200
Nor could there be. Then why were you so keen?
Whose interests were you working for? Did you
Intend to marry a Greek? Was one of them
Related to you? Or some other reason?
They'd send another army here to burn
Your crops? Who do you think believes you?
It was the gold, you might as well admit it,
Gold and your itching palm that killed my son.
I'll make it plainer still. When Troy was winning
And there was still a wall around our city   1210
And Priam lived, and Hector's spear drew blood,
Why didn't you kill him then, if you desired
To further this man's interests, or take him
To the Greeks alive? He was your ward, your care.
But when the sun no longer shone on us
And clouds of smoke announced the fall of Troy,
You killed a friend that came to you for shelter.
And here is more proof of your treachery:
If you were Greece's friend, you should have given
The gold to them – you have admitted   1220
It was his, not yours; for they had need of it,
And had not seen their homes for many years.
But even now you cannot bring yourself
To part with it. It's there still, in your palace.

If you'd cared for the boy as you were bound to
And kept him safe, then I would sing your praises.
True friends reveal themselves in time of trouble;
Prosperity has never lacked a friend.
If you had need of money, he was rich;
His treasure would have been at your command.
1230   Now you have lost a friend in Polydorus,
Your joy in gold has gone, your sons are gone
And you are . . . as you are. I say to you,
Agamemnon, you'll be false if you befriend him.
You'll help a man who has no honesty
Or self-respect; an atheist, a criminal.
And we shall say that you are such another,
Loving his vices. But I'll not abuse my masters.

CHORUS.
Honest causes always give a man
Scope to utter honest arguments.

AGAMEMNON.
1240   I find it hard to judge another's sins
But have to do it. I should be ashamed
To go back on a charge I had accepted.
So hear me. It was not, in my opinion,
To serve the Greeks or me you killed your friend,
But to get his gold into your possession.
Now you are in trouble, so you make excuses.
Killing your friends may come easily to you,
But Greeks find such behaviour criminal.
How could I give a verdict in your favour
1250   Without condemning myself? If you're prepared
To sin, then you must take the consequences.

POLYMESTOR.
Shall I be beaten by a woman and a slave,
And yield my cause to my inferiors?

HECUBA.
Is it not justice, after what you did?

POLYMESTOR.
Oh, my children; oh, my eyes!

HECUBA.

They hurt. You think my son does not hurt me?

POLYMESTOR.

You witch, you take delight in taunting me.

HECUBA.

Why should I not? Revenge is sweet.

POLYMESTOR.

You will not laugh so loudly, when the sea –

HECUBA.

Takes me to Greece? Is that what you would say?   1260

POLYMESTOR.

Swallows you, when you have fallen from the masthead!

HECUBA.

Is someone going to push me overboard?

POLYMESTOR.

No. You will climb the mast of your own will –

HECUBA.

How? Do you mean to say I shall sprout wings?

POLYMESTOR.

You'll turn into a dog with flaming eyes.

HECUBA.

How do you know that I will change my shape?

POLYMESTOR.

Our oracle of Dionysus told me.

HECUBA.

And did not mention what would fall on you?

POLYMESTOR.

If I had known, you never would have tricked me.

HECUBA.

Shall I die? Or go on living where I fall?   1270

POLYMESTOR.

Die; and your tomb shall have a name –

HECUBA.

To suit my new appearance, I suppose?

POLYMESTOR.
The bitch's monument, a sailor's landmark.

HECUBA.
What do I care? I have punished you.

POLYMESTOR.
Your daughter Cassandra will die too.

HECUBA.
I spit that prophecy back in your face!

POLYMESTOR.
His wife, his treacherous housedog, will kill her.

HECUBA.
May Clytemnestra never be so mad!

POLYMESTOR.
And she will take an axe and kill you too!

AGAMEMNON.
1280   Have you lost your mind? Are you asking for more trouble?

POLYMESTOR.
Kill me; killing waits for you in Argos.

AGAMEMNON.
Away with him! Take him out of my sight!

POLYMESTOR.
You like what I tell you?

AGAMEMNON.
Shut your mouth!

POLYMESTOR.
Shut it for me. I've finished!

AGAMEMNON.
Take him away!
Throw him out on some deserted island.
He's raving. There will be no end to this.

The soldiers drag POLYMESTOR *out.*

Hecuba, come. There are still two bodies
Waiting to be buried. Trojan women, you must go
To your masters' tents. I can feel the wind

That will drive us back to our land again.   1290
Grant us safe voyage home; and let us find
All well there. Let us leave our pains behind.

Exeunt AGAMEMNON *and* HECUBA.

CHORUS.
Come friends, to our tents and to the harbour
To try what our masters impose on us.
Necessity is hard.

Exit CHORUS.

THE WOMEN OF TROY

translated by Don Taylor

Characters

POSEIDON, god of the sea
ATHENE, goddess of wisdom
HECUBA, widow of Priam, King of Troy
CASSANDRA, their daughter, a prophetess
ANDROMACHE, their daughter-in-law, widow of Hector
TALTHYBIUS, a Greek officer
MENELAUS, King of Sparta
HELEN, his wife
CHORUS of Trojan women, captured, and soon to be
enslaved
ASTYANAX, a small boy, Hector's son (non-speaking)
GREEK SOLDIERS, guards

The ruins of Troy. HECUBA *is lying face down and quite still.*
Enter the god POSEIDON.

POSEIDON.

    I have come here from the bottom of the sea,
    The salt waters of the Aegean, where the daughters
    Of Nereus, fifty sea-nymphs in chorus,
    Circle in their intricate and beautiful dance.
    My name is Poseidon. I am a god.
    I built this city – with Apollo I built it –
    Every stone we laid, every tower,
    Even the walls we dressed and levelled
    With plumb line and mason's square.
    So I've always had a particular love
    For this city of the Phrygians: and look at it now:
    A smoking ruin, devastated by the power
    Of the Greek war machine. A Phocian inventor   10
    By the name of Epeios, who lived on Parnassus,
    With skills he learned from Athene, and probably
    With her help, designed and built
    A horse, whose capacious belly was pregnant
    With armed commandos, and managed to get it –
    Together with its murderous payload –
    Inside the walls; so that no one
    In the future will ever forget the stratagem
    That goes by the name of the Wooden Horse,
    Nor the ferocious strike force it concealed.
    And now, the temple gardens are deserted,
    And puddles of blood smear the sanctuaries
    Of all the gods. King Priam lies dead
    On the steps of the temple of Zeus protector
    Of the city. More gold than can be counted
    And anything soldiers can loot finds its way
    Down to the Greek ships; and all
    They're waiting for now is a following wind,   20
    So that after ten years, and ten sowing seasons,
    They can joyfully set eyes on their wives and children,
    These Greeks, who brought an army to sack Troy!
    As for me, I have been defeated

Too, by Athene, and Hera, goddesses
Who supported the Greeks, and who, between them,
Have utterly devastated this city of the Phrygians.
So now I too shall desert famous Troy,
And all those altars and temples raised
In my name. For when a town
Is destroyed, and becomes a wilderness,
All worship ceases, and there's no longer
Anything left worth a god's consideration.
Now the riverbank of the Scamander echoes
With the screams and moans of captured women,
As various Greek lords draw lots for them
And they become their slaves. Arcadian
30   Princes draw some, Thessalians others,
And the Princes of Athens, Theseus' descendants,
Get their share. All the women
Of Troy who've not yet been allocated
Are in this building here. They've been reserved
For the leaders of the Greek army. And with them,
A prisoner, like the rest – and quite right too –
Is the Spartan daughter of Tyndareus, Helen.
But to see the true face of misery
You need to look no further than the poor creature
Lying here, in front of the gate, Hecuba,
Whose unnumbered tears match the numberless dead
40   She grieves for. Her daughter, Polyxena,
Has been secretly and brutally murdered
At the tomb of Achilles, in payment for his death.
Priam is dead too, and her sons by him:
And her daughter Cassandra, the frenzied visionary
Whom even the god Apollo left
Untouched as a virgin, Agamemnon
Intends to make his concubine –
A dangerous business, best kept in the dark,
That flouts all religious feeling.
Well then, most prosperous of cities, home
Of the rich and fortunate, time to say goodbye!
Shining towers and citadels, farewell for ever.
If Pallas Athene, daughter of Zeus,

Had not determined to destroy you, your foundations
Would be as firm and solid as ever they were.

Enter ATHENE.

ATHENE.
May our old antagonism be forgotten?
I have something to say to you, brother of my father,
Great god as you are, whom other gods honour.   50

POSEIDON.
Certainly it may. We are blood relations,
Queen Athene, and that warms my heart.

ATHENE.
You are generous to say so. The question at issue
Is a matter of equal concern to us both.

POSEIDON.
What is it? Some new dispensation from the gods?
From Zeus himself? Or some other divinity?

ATHENE.
No, it concerns Troy, on whose ground we now stand.
I want to make a pact: join your power to mine.

POSEIDON.
Is that so? You pity your ancient enemy now,
You see her a smoke blackened ruin, do you?   60

ATHENE.
That's not the point. First, give me your answer.
Will you join me, and help to carry out my plan?

POSEIDON.
By all means. Though I'd be glad to know what it is.
Are you helping the Greeks now, or the Trojans?

ATHENE.
My former enemies, the Trojans, will be comforted.
I shall make the Greeks' return home a disaster.

POSEIDON.
A somewhat cavalier change of mind, surely?
Are you usually so casual whom you love or hate?

ATHENE.
   Haven't you heard. I've been insulted, my temple
                                               desecrated!

POSEIDON.
70   Yes, I know. When Ajax dragged Cassandra from sanctuary.

ATHENE.
   The Greeks didn't punish him. Not even a reprimand.

POSEIDON.
   When your power had enabled them to bring Troy to its
                                                      knees!

ATHENE.
   I shall punish them for that. With your help.

POSEIDON.
   I'm entirely at your service. What can I do?

ATHENE.
   I want their voyage home to be complete disaster.

POSEIDON.
   Before they set sail? Or out at sea?

ATHENE.
   When they've left Troy and are nearing home.
   Zeus has promised me a savage hail storm,
   Torrential rain and gale force winds
   In the middle of the night. And he's given me
80   The use of his thunderbolts, to strike the Greek ships
   With lightning, and burn them at sea.
   Your task will be to make the Aegean
   Heave with mountainous waves, every third wave even
                                                      higher

   Than the rest, and swirl and eddy the salt waters
   With dangerous whirlpools, and fill
   The whole bay of Euboea with floating corpses
   So thick you could walk on them. So that the Greeks
   Will learn their lesson, and in future, respect
   My temples, and fear the power of the gods.

POSEIDON.
   Athene, you need not waste more words,

I shall do that with pleasure. The whole Aegean
From the shores of Mykonos and the rocks of Delos
To Skyros and Lemnos and the headlands of Capheria   90
And the open salt sea, I shall whip up to a foam,
So that the number of the drowned will be beyond
                        counting.
You get off to Olympus now, get hold
Of the thunderbolts, and watch your opportunity
When the Greek fleet casts off for home.
When a man sacks a town and destroys everything,
Even sacred temples and the tombs of the dead,
He's asking for trouble. The same destruction
Sooner or later, will fall on his own head.

Exeunt ATHENE *and* POSEIDON.

HECUBA.

Lift up your head from the dust,
Heave up from the earth
The weight of your misery, you whom the gods have
                        cursed.
Troy has ceased to exist: and we, by birth   100
Troy's Kings and Queens, rule nothing now.
The old life is gone, old gods, old hearth
And home, destroyed. We must endure it, flow
With the stream, let the new wind fill our sail,
Not breast a running tide with our fragile prow.
Oh, weep, weep, for my burning home, howl
For my children dead, for my husband dead, the boast
Of my noble family, empty as a sail when the winds fall.

Some agonies are beyond telling,
And some must be told.   110
Let my stretched limbs shake with it then, this keening,
On my rack of pain, my bed of cold
Stone. My temples are throbbing, my head
Will burst, my heart shatters the walled
Prison of my breast. Oh to sway, flow, lifted
By the gentle rocking of a boat, to keep time
With the dirge I must sing now, the song of the dead,
My threnody of tears. This is the only theme

120   For the black clad Muse of the destroyed, no dancing
        Can express it, dissonant music, harsh rhyme.

        Oh you ships, whose sharp prows
        Cut the purple sea
        As your oars pulled in a cloud of spray
        From the sanctuary
        Of the harbours of Greece, till your bows
        Grounded in the bay of Troy, sad Troy,
        Ominous your flutes' bleak song,
        Your pipes' deathlike cry
        As on taut Egyptian cables you swung
130   At your moorings at Troy, sad Troy,
        Like hunters on the scent
        Of Menelaus' Helen, born to dismay
        Her brother Castor, and bring
        Shame to the banks of Eurotas, you brought
        Death to Priam whose seed bred fifty sons, a headlong
        Fall to suffering Hecuba, and a broken heart.

        Look at me now, throned in the dust
        By Agamemnon's tentflap,
140   An old woman, dragged as a slave
        From my home, all hope
        Plundered from my god-cursed
        Ravaged grey head, with no reprieve
        From my punishment of everlasting sorrow.
        Weep, wives of the bronze armoured Trojans, grieve
        For your heroes dead, daughters, harrow
        The clouds with your tears for husbands lost!
        Troy is burning.
        Like the mother bird at her plundered nest,
        My song has become a scream, no music can I borrow
        From the stately dance or the solemn psalming
150   To the gods of Troy I sang among the women, nor the slow
        Rhythm I began, Priam's sceptre in my hand, when I led
                                        the dancing.

        Enter the CHORUS.

        CHORUS.
        Hecuba, did you shout aloud,

Or was it a howl of agony?
How far did it carry? Through the walls we heard
A sound that made us shiver in our misery
As we hid in the ruins, wretched women of Troy,
Facing a life of slavery.

HECUBA.

My women, my girls, already the Greeks deploy
Their ships, their hands reach for the oars!   160

CHORUS.

No, no! Will they really drag us away
From our homes, and ship us overseas to theirs?

HECUBA.

I know nothing: but sense that the worst will come.

CHORUS.

I can't bear it! Soon we will hear them shout,
'Get moving, you Trojan women, hey, slave,
Kiss your home goodbye, and now, move out
And get on board. We're sailing for home!'

HECUBA.

But not Cassandra, not her, dear heaven, leave
That child inside, my god-crazed daughter   170
In her visionary ecstasy.
Don't let the Greek soldiers deport her,
Not a poor mad girl. How can I grieve
More than I do, is there more pain for me?
Oh Troy, you are lost.
We all leave you now. And whose misery
Is greater, the dead, whose day is passed,
Or the living, who must live in slavery?

CHORUS.

I'm so frightened, look, I'm shaking with terror!
I crept from Agamemnon's tents, dear Queen,
When I heard you cry out. What new horror
Must I suffer? Surely the Greeks don't mean
To kill me here? Are they mustering at their ships,   180
Getting ready to row, in groups by the stern?

HECUBA.
My children, a blasted mind never sleeps.
I came out here at dawn. But there's no relief.

CHORUS.
Is there any decision? No message from the Greeks
About the slave allocation? Who'll be master of my grief?

HECUBA.
It won't be long now till you hear the worst.

CHORUS.
I can't bear it. Who will it be, which lord
Of the Greeks will carry me over the sea
To Argos, or Phthia, or some bleak island
190 Far, far from Troy, one of the accursed!

HECUBA.
Oh you gods, where in my misery
Shall I go, what corner of the earth
Shall I burden with my old age,
Like a drone in the hive, or an image of death
Still in the flesh: a shadow from the country
Of forgotten shadows? I'll be a concierge,
They'll sit me at the outer gate,
Or in the nursery with the children, in the entourage
Of some Greek Princeling: I, who in Troy held my state
As a Queen, half divine, with Kings to pay me homage!

CHORUS.
Oh the pity of it, the pity! What words,
What howling, can give tongue to a pain
No animal could endure! Never again in the shadow
Of Mount Ida will these hands of mine
Pass the shuttle back and forth between the threads
200 As I sit at my loom. For the last time I harrow
My heart with the sight of my dead sons,
The last time, before greater sorrow
Overwhelms me, and my slavery begins:
Perhaps forced into the bed of some loathsome Greek,
– Gods curse such a night, and the evil
Powers that bring me to it! – Or maybe my slave's back

Will break drawing holy water from Peirene. O, Athens,
God-favoured city of Theseus, may I come to you, not
                                                      grovel
By the turbulent Eurotas, at Menelaus' mercy, part of
                                                      Helen's   210
Loathed household, under the Troy-sacker's heel!

I have heard men say that the foothills
Of Peneius, beneath Olympus, are famous for their wealth
And the fertility of their green fields.
There, of all places on earth,
Would be my second choice, after the sacred halls
Of Athens. And the land of Mount Etna, which scalds
Its slopes with Hephaestos' fire, the mountain
                                            homeland   220
Of Sicily, across the strait from Tunis, holds
Pride of place for integrity, and is renowned
For its brave men. And there is a secluded valley
They tell me, watered by a beautiful river
Named Crathis, close to the Ionian sea,
Whose dark streams, like hair, as they flow become
                                            reddened
Into the richest gold. Its springs are sacred, and for ever
Blessed with plenty is that valley, breeding heroes hardened
For war. I'd be happy enough to live there.

But look: a staff officer of the Greek army   230
Has some news for us. I can see him hurrying
At a brisk march in our direction.
What will he tell us? What more worth saying?
The Dorian Greeks have reduced us to slavery.

Enter TALTHYBIUS *with guards.*

TALTHYBIUS.
Hecuba . . . you are not unaware that on many occasions
As officer in charge of negotiations, or outlining our
                                            proposals,
I have come here from the Greek camp. So I'm no
                                            stranger –
Talthybius, you may remember me – I have some news
                                            for you.

HECUBA.
This is it my dears, what we've feared for so long . . .

TALTHYBIUS.
You've been allocated to your masters . . . if that's what
240   you're afraid of.

HECUBA.
Aieeeee . . . ! Where then? Phthia? Somewhere else in
                                                                    Thessaly?
Or is it to be Thebes, Cadmus' city?

TALTHYBIUS.
You are allocated separately: not all together.

HECUBA.
So who goes to whom? Which of the women of Troy
Has been lucky, and will dance for joy?

TALTHYBIUS.
The fact is . . . ask one at a time, not all at once . . .

HECUBA.
My poor child, who has won her, Cassandra,
My god-stricken daughter?

TALTHYBIUS.
Agamemnon made a special note of her, and took her for
                                                                    himself.

HECUBA.
Ah God! – Must she be slave to his Spartan wife,
250   Her bondservant for life?

TALTHYBIUS.
Not at all, she's for him. In darkness. In his bed.

HECUBA.
What! She is a consecrated virgin, Apollo's nun.
Lifelong virginity she was promised, by Zeus' golden-haired
                                                                    son!

TALTHYBIUS.
He wants her *because* she's sacred. He's shot through with
                                                                    lust.

HECUBA.
Throw away the keys of the temple, my child,

Strip off your sacred habit,
Trample the flowers on the ground!

TALTHYBIUS.
Now look here, to be a King's mistress is no bad thing.

HECUBA.
And my youngest child, where's she? You tore her
from my arms. 260

TALTHYBIUS.
Polyxena, you mean . . . or is it someone else?

HECUBA.
Yes. Who gets her by the luck of the draw?

TALTHYBIUS.
She is to serve Achilles, at his tomb.

HECUBA.
Dear heavens, must a child I bore
Be a servant at a tomb?
Is this a custom among you Greeks, my friend, or some
new law?

TALTHYBIUS.
Consider your child fortunate. All's well with her.

HECUBA.
What does that mean? She is alive? Is she?

TALTHYBIUS.
Her fate is settled. All her troubles are over. 270

HECUBA.
And the wife of Hector, the incomparable warrior?
What happens to Andromache? What Greek draws her?

TALTHYBIUS.
She was chosen specially, by the son of Achilles.

HECUBA.
And whose slave am I? Grey-haired Hecuba.
Who needs a stick as a third foot to support her?

TALTHYBIUS.
Odysseus, King of Ithaca, drew you, as his slave.

HECUBA.
Ah . . . pain, and still more pain . . . !
Let me tear the hair in handfuls from my head,
280   Plough my face with my nails, till the wrinkles run red,
Still agony, and greater agony . . . !
I've drawn the shortest straw, even worse than I feared –
To be the slave of a man without morality,
A liar, a deceiver, to whom laws of gods and men
Mean nothing, whose animal appetite
Savages all decency, and whose double tongue
Twists truth into lies, friendship to enmity!
Weep for me, women of Troy, this last lottery of fate
290   Will be the end of me. Veil me in shadows, I belong
In the deepest pit of misery.

CHORUS.
We know the worst now for you, dear Queen,
But which of the Greeks has my future in his power?

TALTHYBIUS.
All right you men, guard detachment,
Go in there and bring Cassandra out.
And move it! When I've handed her over
To the Commander in Chief, I can take the rest
Of you enslaved women to your masters,
According to the allocation. Hey . . . ! What's that?
Have they got lighted torches in there?
Are they setting fire to the place, or what?
300   These Trojan women, just because we're taking them
From their homes across to Argos . . . dear God,
Are they trying to commit suicide in there,
Setting light to themselves? To tell the truth,
These are a proud people. In circumstances like these
They don't take kindly to humiliation.
All right, open up, open up in there!
It may suit their dignity to insult the Greeks
Like this, but I shall have to carry the can.

HECUBA.
No, no one's setting fire to anything. It's my poor
Manic daughter, Cassandra, she's running out here . . . !

Enter CASSANDRA.

CASSANDRA.

Hold it up, the torch, take it, let it flame
Higher, oh hold it higher!
Let it burn everything sacred to Apollo!
Hymen, god of marriage, hallow   310
The bridegroom and his desire,
And bless me, the bride, and my new home,
The royal bedroom of Argos! Hymen, bless my wedding,
As I glorify you with my singing!

You, Mother, you sing
For my father murdered, our city
Destroyed, a sad keening song,
Dirge for our country!
But I fired these torches, illuminating   320
My holy wedding feast, a blazing light
To celebrate the marriage of virginity,
And Hymen, god of lust, and the dark night
Of Hecate, the consecrated virgin's deflowering!

Begin the dance then, let our feet take wing, float higher
In ecstasy, ah, ecstasy,
As if this were a feast in celebration
Of my father's good luck, the zenith of his fortune!
This ritual dance is holy,
God Apollo, lead us to your altar
Under the laurel tree, where I dedicated my life.   330
Now, Hymen, god of marriage, make me a good wife!
Dance, Mother, dance with me!
You should be laughing. Let your flying feet
Keep time with mine, whirling in ecstasy
Faster and faster, and shout,
Shout, Mother, the old songs of matrimony!
Sing, sing, women of Troy,
Put on your most glittering dresses, celebrate
The virgin's lucky marriage! I shall enjoy   340
A husband bedded by the hand of destiny!

CHORUS.

Dear Queen, your daughter's possessed! Hold on to her,
Or she'll dance her way right down to the Greek camp.

HECUBA.

    Oh Hephaestos, you gave flaming torches
    To mortal men, to carry in honour of marriage.
    But these torches are a grotesque parody
    Of everything I hoped for for my daughter.
    Oh my dear child, when I dreamed of your marriage
    I never imagined it would be like this, thrust
    At spear-point into some Greek's bed
    As a slave of his lust! Give me the torch,
    Poor child, you're not fit to carry anything burning
    In your half-crazed state. All this suffering
    Hasn't brought you to your senses, has it,
350   You're just as much a poor mad thing
    As you ever were. Here, women of Troy,
    Take these torches back inside,
    And let her dreadful parody of a wedding song
    Be drowned by the sound of your tears.

CASSANDRA.

    Mother, you must cover my hair with flowers,
    A victory crown to celebrate my triumph,
    Marrying a King. You must lead me to him,
    And if I don't seem overwhelmed at the prospect,
    Take no notice, give me a good shove,
    Force me, by violence, if you have to!
    Because, if the god Apollo exists
    At all, then Agamemnon, the world famous leader
    Of the Greeks, will find me more destructive
    As a wife than ever Helen was!
    Because I'll kill him, and destroy his whole family
360   In return for my father and brothers destroyed.
    But that's enough. No more now. Some things
    Are best passed over in silence. Why should I sing
    Prophetic songs about the axe that will sever my neck,
    And some other necks too? Or the son
    Murdering the mother, or the total annihilation
    Of the House of Atreus, all the rich fruit
    Which the tree of my marriage will bear!
    Look! Let me tell you. This city of Troy

Is far happier than the whole nation of the Greeks:
And I'll prove it to you. Yes, I'm possessed,
Inspired, call it what you like. But,
For one moment, let me stand outside
This god-drunken ecstasy, and speak
As though my voice were my own. These Greeks,
For the sake of one woman, and one moment
Of uncontrollable lust, sent a hunting party
To track down Helen, to smoke her out,
And it cost them tens of thousands dead!
And their oh-so-wise Commander, to achieve   370
What he hated most, lose what he loved most,
Giving up the pleasure of his family and children
For the sake of his brother Menelaus' wife,
Who was not dragged away from her home by force,
But ran away and was unfaithful, because she wanted to!
And when they came here, to the banks of Scamander,
These Greeks, then they began to die,
And they kept on dying. And for what reason?
They weren't being robbed, they weren't being invaded,
They didn't see the towers and battlements
Of their homeland being occupied.
And those who became the war god's victims
Had forgotten what their children looked like.   380
They weren't washed and shrouded and laid to rest
By their wives' loving hands: and now
Their bodies lie forgotten in a foreign country.
And things were no better at home. Their women
Died in the loneliness of widowhood,
Their fathers became childless old men,
Who had bred up their sons . . . for nothing,
To lie in a distant country, with no relatives
To honour them and make sacrifices at their graves.
Oh yes, the whole Greek nation
Has a great deal to thank their army for!
There were other things too, terrible things,
Things better left unsaid, not fit
To be spoken by ,he tongue of a consecrated virgin.
But our Trojans! What a contrast there! They won

The greatest of all glories. They died
Fighting for their fatherland! And if an enemy spear
Found its target, and in a moment made a living man
Into a corpse, that man was carried from the field
By his own platoon, the earth that covered him
Was the sacred soil of the land of his fathers.
The hands that wrapped him in his shroud
Were the right hands, according to the customs
390 Of burial in our country. And those Trojan soldiers
Who didn't die in battle, lived at home,
Spending every day with their wives and children,
The simplest of pleasures, denied to the Greeks.
And when you grieve for Hector, remember this.
Listen to me now, because this is the truth.
He proved, in action, he was the greatest of men.
And now he is gone. Dead. And all this
Has been the direct result of the coming of the Greeks.
Supposing they had stayed at home? We would never
Have seen Hector's glory, all that brightness
Would have remained hidden! And Paris. He married
The daughter of Zeus. If he hadn't married her
Who would have sung songs in his honour in our palaces?
400 Any sensible man must hate war,
He does his best to avoid it. But if it should come,
Even if it should end like this, it is no shame
For a city, indeed, it is a crown of honour
To die nobly, with dignity. The really shameful thing
Is to die dishonourably, ignobly, without pride.
So you see, Mother, you need not pity our country,
Nor weep for my 'marriage'. Think of those
We hate the most, you and I,
And be sure, that by means of this marriage of mine
I shall destroy them.

CHORUS.
You make light of all these horrors, and laugh at your own
                                                    pain,

The disasters you prophesy are fantasies. They won't
                                                    happen.

TALTHYBIUS.

If it weren't for the fact that your devotion
To Apollo has left you mentally disturbed,
You would be severely punished for cursing our
                                    Generals
Like that, just as they are about to set sail.
It's surprising how often those that seem the wisest   410
And of the highest regard, do things which show them
To be something a good deal less. The greatest,
The most powerful General in the Greek army,
The son of Atreus himself, has let uncontrollable lust
For this madwoman get the better of him.
I'm a poor man. But there's no way
I'd let her anywhere near my bed!
And as for you. Since you're out of your mind,
We'll let your insults to the Greeks, and ridiculously
Overblown compliments to your own side, float away
On the breeze, with the breath that uttered them.
Come on then, follow me, it's time
You were getting on board. What a lovely bride   420
For my Commander-in-Chief! And you, Hecuba,
You can follow us down where Laertes' son
Comes to get you. You'll be his wife's slave,
Penelope. She's a decent, sensible woman.
You won't find a Greek at Troy to say otherwise.

CASSANDRA.

What a clever fellow he is,
This underling! Officers of your kind
Are always hated by everyone, lackeys,
Slaves yourselves, doing great men's dirty work.
You say my mother will be taken from here
To Odysseus' palace. But what about the words
Of Apollo, spoken through my mouth?
They say that she will die here,
And other things, about her death,   430
Too terrible to be spoken. And as for Odysseus,
What can I say about his sufferings,
Except that what I suffer, and what Troy suffers

Will one day seem like a golden age
To him? He will add ten further years
To the ten years he has spent here
Before he reaches his fatherland,
And he'll reach it alone. He will have endured
The terrifying passage through the rocky gorge
Of Charybdis, and the mountain pastures
Of the Cyclops, who eats human flesh.
On the Ligurian coast he will meet the witch
Circe, who turns men into pigs;
He will be shipwrecked more than once
In the open sea, and have to face
The seductive desire for oblivion
In the drugged land of the Lotus eaters,
And the sacred oxen of the sun god,
440   Whose slaughtered and jointed flesh will moan
Like a human being in pain, a sound
To strike terror into Odysseus' breast.
Finally, to cut short this catalogue of horrors,
He will pass through Hell, while still alive,
And after crossing the marshes of the lake of the dead,
When he reaches Ithaca, he will find his old home
Torn apart by troubles, ten thousand of them!
But why should we waste our breath on the sorrows that lie
in wait
For Odysseus? That arrow has left the string, but not yet
Hit the bull. Take me then, to marry my bridegroom
In the very doorway of Hell! In the dead of night they'll
come
To bury you, vilest, filthiest of men, as though
The daylight were ashamed to see you, the great Greek
leader brought low
Who dreamed of mounting so high! Me too, my naked flesh
Will be thrown into a rocky gulley, where the storm waters
rush
Close by my bridegroom's grave! Wild animals will eat
Apollo's consecrated priestess. My crown of flowers,
450   my white

Robe of the most beautiful of the gods, and all the ritual of
                                        Dionysus,
Goodbye to all of it, the feasting and celebrations, so
                                        precious
To me! Tear them all off, and my skin too in strips, let the
                                        wind
Carry them back to the god of prophecy, while my flesh is
                                        still untouched.
Where is the General's flagship? Which way must I go?
                                        Who
Could wait for the wind that fills her sails more eagerly than
                                        I do?
One of the avenging furies, dragged from the ruins of Troy!
Goodbye Mother. No tears. Oh land of my fathers, dead
                                        brothers who lie
Under this earth, Father who sired me, soon, soon we'll
                                        meet,
Short, oh short my journey, in the house of the dead, and
                                        you'll greet
Me with joy for the victory I bring: the family at
                                whose hands Troy died   460
And all her people perished, the House of Atreus,
                                        destroyed!

Exit CASSANDRA *with the guards.*

CHORUS.
Where are Hecuba's women? Your venerable Queen
Has fainted, she's collapsed, and lies speechless on the
                                        ground.
Don't let her just lie there, you bitches, an old woman
Fallen flat on her face. Get her up on her feet!

HECUBA.
No, leave me alone. Your kindness, my girls,
Is no kindness to me. Let me lie here
Just as I fell. What I am suffering,
And have suffered, what I will suffer yet,
Is more than enough to make anyone fall
And never get up again. Oh you gods,
What good were you to us? Betrayers!

470   And yet people still call upon gods
When bad luck, or history, has flattened them
And the whole of their world has collapsed.
So let me tell you how fortunate I was,
Born lucky, to heighten the tragedy
Of what has happened to me now. I was royal
By birth, and I married a King. My sons
Excelled, not merely because I bore so many,
But because they were the best among the Phrygians.
What's more, they were Trojans, and such Trojans
As no Greek woman or barbarian
Could ever boast of bearing. And I saw
Every one of them slaughtered by the swords
And spears of the Greeks! By their open graves

480   I have stood, and cut my hair in mourning
To cast upon their bodies; and so many bitter tears
I have wept for their father, Priam. No one
Told me of his death, no one
Brought me the news. With my own eyes
I saw him hacked down on the altar steps
Of our holiest temple, and the whole city sacked
As the Greeks ran riot; all the daughters I brought up
With such care, to make them fit brides for Princes,
I saw them snatched from my arms, their good breeding
Wasted on brutal soldiery and foreigners.
There's no hope they'll ever see me again
Or that I will ever see them. And now,
Like the keystone to my arch of misery,
In my old age I must go to Greece

490   To finish my life as a slave. And what work
They will give me, a woman of my years,
To be a gatekeeper, looking after the keys,
Me, the mother of Hector, or a kitchen skivvy
Kneading the bread dough. I won't sleep
On a royal mattress any more, the floor
Will be good enough for my bony back
And wasted flesh; worn out, second hand
Dresses will do for me, rags even,
The sort that well bred women never see

Let alone wear, they will have to make do
For my worn out, second hand body.
Dear gods, what a terrible retribution,
All that has happened to me, and will happen,
Because of that one woman and her love affair!
Cassandra, my child, what violation will end   500
Your consecrated virginity, that mystic ecstasy
You shared with Dionysus, and all the gods?
And you, my poor girl, Polyxena,
Where are you now? None of my children
Neither sons nor daughters – and there were so many of
                                                        them –
Can give me so much as a helping hand
In my misery. They are all gone.
So why try to help me up? What for?
What have I to look forward to? Well. Take my hand
And lead me step by step – these feet of mine –
So used to deep carpets, all the luxury of Troy,
They belong to a slave now. Bring me to my bed,
My straw palliasse and stone pillow,
Throw me down there on my face
And let these tears, my torturers, whip me senseless.
Wealth, good fortune, it's all worth nothing.
There is no happiness. The lucky ones are dead.   510

CHORUS.

Teach me, gods of song, some harsh lament
Dissonant with tears and howls,
Help me to sing Troy's sorrows, invent
New sounds for my grief: the Greek horse on wheels
Has ruined me, brought me to the edge of the grave
Made me a slave.
Unguarded they left it, by the main gate,
Its gold cheek pieces gleaming,   520
And from its belly the clash of armour plate
Rumbled like thunder, muffled and threatening.
So we ran to the rock of the citadel
The whole population, shouting,
'Come out everybody, all

Our troubles are over, wheel
This wooden offering for Zeus' daughter,
Athene of Troy, inside the wall!'
And who ran from their houses the faster,
The young men or the old? All high
On the singing and the joy, as they laid hands on the
          monster
That was more than it seemed, and would doom them all to
530   die.

Then it seemed the whole nation of the Phrygians ran
To the gates, eager to bring
That smooth planed icon of mountain pine
And the Greek ambush within it, as an offering
To the virgin who drives the immortal horses of heaven –
For the Trojans, destruction.
Roped with cables of twisted flax
They heaved it, like a black ship,
540 To the stone shrine at the heart of the temple complex
Of Pallas Athene – altars soon to drip
And smooth floors run slippery with Trojan blood.
Then the melodious African pipe
Honeyed the air, as the dark hood
Of night enfolded Troy. In celebration
After the day's exhaustion, the whole city was singing,
Dancing feet stamping in exhilaration
To the rhythm of young girls' voices, flickering
Torches casting puddles of light
In the darkened palaces, and on the faces sleeping,
And in eyes wide awake and glittering in the pitch
550   dark night.

At that time in our great hall
With the others, I was singing
All our favourite songs to Artemis, Zeus' daughter,
Virgin of the mountains, and joining in the dancing;
When suddenly I heard a terrible howl,
The unmistakable sound of murder,
A terrified scream rising from the streets of the whole
City. Children grabbed hold of their mothers'

Skirts, their pale hands plucked at her gown,
Fluttering with fear. The god of war   560
Had sprung his trap, the ambush strategy
Worked perfectly, thanks to Pallas Athene, whose power
Secretly inspired it. The Trojans were cut down
In their own homes, in sanctuary, beheaded where they
                                                          lay
Sleeping, a whole generation of women raped in their
                                                          own
Bedrooms, breeding bastards for the Greeks, desolation
                                                   for Troy.

Look, Hecuba, they're bringing Andromache
In a Greek baggage waggon. Her bosom is heaving   570
With sobs, as she grasps Hector's son, Astyanax, clinging
To her breasts, as they rise and fall like a bank of oars in
                                                      the sea.

Enter ANDROMACHE *and her young son,* ASTYANAX,
wheeled in on top of a baggage waggon loaded with spoils.

The son of Achilles will hang up Troy's plundered
                                                   splendour
As a trophy under some Phthian temple roof!

ANDROMACHE.
My Greek masters are only taking what's theirs.

HECUBA.
Aiee, Aiee!

ANDROMACHE.
                    Don't sing *my* victory song!

HECUBA.
Agony!

ANDROMACHE.
                    The agonies are all mine.

HECUBA.
Oh Zeus!

ANDROMACHE.
                    Hard learned, to be suffered long.   580

HECUBA.
My children!

ANDROMACHE.
                    No longer. Grown old in tears.

HECUBA.
  All our happiness. Troy, our city. Gone.

ANDROMACHE.
  Into misery.

HECUBA.
                    My children, my heroic sons!

ANDROMACHE.
  All gone, all gone.

HECUBA.
                    What grief is like mine?

ANDROMACHE.
  My suffering.

HECUBA.
                    The sobbing, the moans.

ANDROMACHE.
  Of our city.

HECUBA.
                    Ruined. Smoke blackened stone.

ANDROMACHE.
  My husband! Where are you? I need you now. Save me!

HECUBA.
  You're calling for a dead man. My firstborn son
  Is in Hades, and I am in misery.

ANDROMACHE.
590 Protect me now, as you've always done.

HECUBA.
  Oh my Priam, whom the Greeks barbarously killed!

ANDROMACHE.
  Old man, great King, princely father,
  Your sons were famous throughout the world.

HECUBA.
  Let me sleep in the arms of death for ever.

ANDROMACHE.
 So bitter, these longings.
HECUBA.
                    Sharp pains now, and sorrows unceasing.
ANDROMACHE.
 For the city we have lost.
HECUBA.
                    And miseries ever increasing.
ANDROMACHE.
 The gods always hated us. Their malice spared your son.
 So that his contemptible marriage should bring ruin
 To the citadel of Troy! Now in bloody pieces he's lying
 For the vultures, in Pallas' temple. Our slavery is his
                                        doing!   600
HECUBA.
 Troy, mother of us all!
ANDROMACHE.
                    Tears blind me. Deserted. A ruin.
HECUBA.
 This pitiful end.
ANDROMACHE.
                    The house my children were born in.
HECUBA.
 I've lost my home. I've lost my children. Everything.
 No grief can encompass what I feel. No funeral song.
 Flow, tears, for a city, and family, shattered past hoping.
 Only the dead shed no tears. They are beyond weeping.
CHORUS.
 Suffering people find some comfort in tears.
 To give voice to grief is a kind of pleasure.
ANDROMACHE.
 Oh Hecuba, mother of the son who speared   610
 So many of these Greeks, do you see what they are doing?
HECUBA.
 I see what the gods are doing, making monuments
 Of worthless men, and demolishing the good.

ANDROMACHE.
  We are loot, my son and I, soldiers' plunder,
  Born royal, and made slaves! The whole world's
                                    overturned.

HECUBA.
  Necessity is logical, and merciless. Cassandra
  Has just been torn from my arms by force.

ANDROMACHE.
  No, no more. I can't bear it . . .
  So some second Ajax flatters his masculinity
  By dragging off your daughter. But . . . there's worse pain
                                    to come.

HECUBA.
620 Of course there is. There's no end to pain.
  The next horror will always be worse than the last.

ANDROMACHE.
  She's dead. Your daughter, Polyxena. Murdered
  At Achilles' tomb, as a sacrifice to the dead.

HECUBA.
  And it is . . . So that's what Talthybius meant,
  The truth his diplomatic evasion concealed.

ANDROMACHE.
  I saw it with my own eyes. I got down from the cart,
  Cut down the body, covered it with her dress.

HECUBA.
  My poor child . . . ritually murdered, filthy,
  Sacrilege . . . oh my poor girl, butchered like an
                                    animal . . . !

ANDROMACHE.
630 Anyway she's dead, however it happened,
  And she's happier dead than I am living.

HECUBA.
  No, no one is happier dead. The living
  At least have hope. To be dead is to be nothing.

ANDROMACHE.
  Dear Mother, listen. You are my mother too,

Even though you didn't give me birth; listen
And draw some comfort from what I'm saying.
To be dead is the same as never to have been born.
But to die is better than a life of agony,
Because the dead feel nothing, and no pain
Can touch them any more. Whereas someone whose life
Has been prosperous and lucky, and is then overwhelmed
By disasters, knows what it's like to have been happy,
And is heartbroken to be excluded from that

paradise . . .   640
For your child, it's as though she had never seen
The light of day, she's dead, and knows nothing
Of her suffering now. It's different for me.
Being Hector's wife, I aimed at the highest
A woman could wish for, and I hit the mark.
And now I have lost everything. Living with Hector
I made it my business to be the perfect wife,
Never wanted even to leave his house,
Because that's the certain way to compromise
A woman's reputation, gave up all desire
To go anywhere and was joyfully fulfilled at home.
And even at home, I admitted no fashionable   650
Gossip or women's chatter, but used my intelligence
To improve my own mind, and was content with that.
I lived quietly with my husband, my happiness was obvious
Whenever our eyes met. I knew what things
Were my prerogative, and how to give in gracefully
To his authority in matters that were his.
But my reputation as the ideal wife
Reached the Greek camp, and that ruined me.
As soon as I was captured, Achilles' son
Asked for me as his wife, meaning his whore,
To be a slave in the very house   660
Of the man who murdered my husband . . .
If I drive the memory of my beloved Hector
Out of my mind, and open the doors
Of my heart to the man who owns me now,
I shall betray the love of the dead man,
And mine to him. And if I refuse

To allow this Prince to touch me, I'll provoke
The hatred of the man whose power is total
Over me and mine. They say one night
In bed with a man will convince any woman
And pleasure away her hatred. I spit in the face
Of any woman who forgets her dead husband
To jump into bed with the next one. Dear God,

670 Not even a mare, uncoupled from her old yokefellow
And stablemate will pull in harness willingly!
And animals are supposed to be inferior to men,
With no power to reason or speak their thoughts!
But you, Hector, my love, you had everything
I dreamed of in a husband, in intelligence, good family,
Wealth and courage the greatest of men!
You took me as a virgin from my father's house,
And I gave my body for the first time to you
In our marriage bed. Now you are dead,
And I am to be transported across the sea
To Greece as a prisoner, to be yoked as a slave.

680 And Polyxena, whom you groan and weep for,
Isn't her suffering far less than mine?
You say everyone living has hope. What hope
Have I? I'm not stupid enough to delude
Myself with false expectations, pleasant
Though such comforting daydreams might be . . .

CHORUS.

Your suffering is like mine. Your anguished words
Give voice to my deepest agonies and fears.

HECUBA.

I've never been on board ship in my life,
But I've seen pictures of them, and heard men talking,
So I know that if the storm is not too violent,
And there's some chance of survival, the sailors
Will do everything they can to come through it, hanging on

690 To the tiller, scrambling aloft to the sails,
And bailing out the water for dear life.
But if the waves run higher, and towering rollers
Overwhelm them, they accept the inevitable

And give themselves to the sea. And so do I too.
The gods have drowned me in an ocean of misery.
After so many sorrows, and in such despair,
Words mean nothing. There's nothing left to say.
But you, dear daughter, dry your eyes.
No more grieving for Hector now.
You must forget him. Even your tears
Can't help him now. My advice to you
Is to make much of your new master.   700
Be pleasant, make yourself attractive to him.
That way you will make everyone's captivity
Easier to bear, and your own life more pleasant.
With luck, you may bring up this grandson of mine
To be the saviour of Troy. Sons of yours
May return to the ruins of Ilium one day
And build a new city from the ashes . . .
But look . . . the next chapter is already beginning.
The Greek minion is coming back,
To tell us, no doubt, what the Greek Council
Has finally decided to do with us all.

TALTHYBIUS *returns, with the guards.*

TALTHYBIUS.
Hector's wife, widow of the greatest of the
                                        Trojans . . .
I ask you not to hate me. With the greatest reluctance   710
I must tell you the news, the joint decision
Of the Council of the Greeks and the two sons of Pelops.

ANDROMACHE.
What is it? That sounds like a prelude to disaster.

TALTHYBIUS.
This child. They have decided . . . I don't know how to
                                        say it.

ANDROMACHE.
No, don't take him away . . . ! We have different
                                        masters . . . ?

TALTHYBIUS.
No Greek will ever be his master.

ANDROMACHE.
How . . . ? Is he to be the last of the Trojans? Left here?

TALTHYBIUS.
There is no decent way to say an indecent thing.

ANDROMACHE.
Thank you for your decency . . . but no more bad
news . . .

TALTHYBIUS.
They mean to kill him. That's the worst. Now you know.

ANDROMACHE.
Oh my God . . . ! That sentence is worse than my
720   marriage . . .

TALTHYBIUS.
Odysseus' speech carried the whole Council . . .

ANDROMACHE.
Aieee, Aieee, I can't bear it, I can't . . . !

TALTHYBIUS.
That the son of such a father must not be allowed to grow
up . . .

ANDROMACHE.
May those arguments condemn his own son!

TALTHYBIUS.
And that he should be thrown from the battlements of
Troy.
This has to be. So please be sensible.
Don't hang on to him like that, but bear this pain
Like the Queen you are. There's nothing you can do.
You are quite without any power to prevent it
So don't imagine otherwise. No one can help you.
730   The city is in ruins, your husband dead.
You are quite alone, and believe me
We are capable of dealing with a single woman
If we have to. So don't make a fight of it,
Or kick or struggle, or curse the Greeks.
If you say anything to anger the army

Your child may not be properly buried
And no tears be shed at his grave. But if
You keep quiet, and resign yourself to what must happen,
They might allow you to bury your child
Decently, and treat you with more consideration.

ANDROMACHE.

My darling, my precious, too dangerous to live,   740
Your enemies will kill you, and leave your mother in
                                        misery,
Your father's courage, that saved so many,
Is a death sentence for you. Everything
That made him great for you proves fatal.
Ah, God, when I came into Hector's palace
On that unlucky wedding day,
And that unluckier wedding night,
I thought I would conceive a son to rule
Over the whole of Asia, not a victim
To be callously murdered, butchered by the Greeks!
My dear little boy, are you crying too?
Do you understand what's happening? Why else
Do you hang on to my hand like that, and bury   750
Your timid face in the folds of my dress
Like a bird creeping under his mother's wing?
There is no Hector rising from the grave
With his spear in his hand, coming to save you,
Nor any of your father's brothers, no army
Of Trojans. You must jump from that terrifying height,
Fall, and break your neck, smash the breath in your
                                        mouth
Without pity from anyone! My sweet baby,
So tender in my arms, dearer than all the world
To your mother, the softness of your breath,
The baby smell of your skin . . . ! All for nothing,
My labour pains when you were born, all for nothing   760
When I gave you my breast, and dressed you so tenderly
In your baby clothes, all nothing, all for nothing.
Hold me tight now, hang on to me, for the last time.
I gave you birth, put your arms round my shoulders

And hang on to me, hard, and kiss me, my boy . . .
You Greeks! You have dreamed up such cruelties
Even the barbarians would flinch at! Why
Are you killing this child? What has he done
In his innocence? He's guilty of nothing!
Helen! You Daughter of Tyndareus! You
Are not Zeus' daughter! More fathers than one
You had, and I know their names too!
Destruction, first of all, and Envy and Murder
And Death, and every evil thing

770   That crawls on the face of the earth! Zeus could never
Have fathered you to bring ruin and slaughter
On Greeks and barbarians alike, by thousands!
Die in agony, and be damned for ever,
You and your beautiful eyes, whose inviting looks
Have brought this famous country of Phrygia
To complete destruction! Come on then! Take him!
Carry him away. Throw him down from the walls
If that's what your generals have decided, and then
Make a banquet of his dead body! The gods
Are destroying us all. I can't save
My own child from death! Parcel up
My disgraced body, and throw it on board ship.
It's a fine wedding I'm sailing to
With my poor son left dead at my back!

CHORUS.

780   Poor Troy. Ten thousand men are dead
For one woman, and her hated marriage bed.

TALTHYBIUS.

Come on boy. You must break that embrace
Now, in spite of your mother's agony,
And climb the walls to the highest bluff
That crowns ancestral Troy. At that place,
According to the vote of the Army Committee,
You must give up your life. Take him then.
                              Someone tough
And unthinking they need for this job, without pity
And no scruples. I'm not half hard enough.

HECUBA.

    Poor child, son of my dead son,   790
    To tear you like that from your mother and from me
    Is wicked. How can I suffer
    This, and learn to bear it? What can be done
    To help you now, enduring this? We can only
    Beat our breasts in anguish, tear our hair,
    And that's all we can do. Our city is gone,
    And soon you will be gone too. There is no agony
    We don't already feel, no abyss of pain to discover.

    ANDROMACHE *is dragged out by the guards one way as*
    ASTYANAX *is taken the other.*

CHORUS.

    From the sea-fringed shore of Salamis, the island of
                                         beehives
    That faces the sacred slopes where the first bough
    Of the blue-grey olive was unveiled by Pallas, ancestor of
                              the groves   800
    That sit like a wreath of honour on the shining brow
    Of Athens, came Telamon, Salamis' founder, across the
                                  waves
    Of the Aegean to destroy
    The ancient city of Troy,
    With the archer Heracles, in the distant past
    When Greece first came to Ilium, to bring it to the dust.

    The flower of Hellas he led in his rage for the immortal
                                   horses
    Of Zeus, first promised, then denied. In the calm
    Shallows of Simois they rested their sea-going oars, cast
                               hawsers 810
    To make fast the sterns, while Heracles' mighty arm
    Took the bow from his ship and killed Laomedon, and with
                                flashes
    Of fire like a whirlwind
    Shattered and burned
    The very stones of Apollo's city. Once in the past
    And now again, Greek arms have brought Dardanus' city to
                              the dust.

820   Oh Ganymede, son of Laomedon,
      As you step so delicately among the golden
      Wine cups, pouring the vintage
      For Zeus, enjoying a favourite's privileges,
      What use are you to your city, as it rages
      In flames, and the Greeks bring carnage
      To the land of your birth? Is that the cry
      Of seagulls screaming for their young
      On the sea shore? No. Women of Troy,
830   Wives for their husbands screaming,
      For their dead sons, daughters weeping desperately
      For mothers too old to live slaves for long.
      Your pools for freshwater swimming, that trackway
      Where you always loved to go running,
      All obliterated now. While you were reclining
      Serene in your youthful beauty
      By the throne of Zeus, the Greeks were destroying
840   Troy's people and Priam's city.

      Love, consuming love, once came
      To the palace of Dardanus, Laomedon's home.
      The gods themselves were trembling
      With the excitement of it, and Troy
      Seemed promised an immortal destiny
      At the Olympian wedding
      Of Tithonus with Aurora, goddess of the dawn.
      No further reproach will pass my lips
      Against Zeus or his doings. What's done is done.
      But the pure light of morning
850   That cheers everyone, saw destruction
      Dawn on our city, saw our citadels collapse;
      And yet, Aurora herself had a Trojan
      Husband in her bed, was breeding
      Children by him, after abducting
      Him in her four-horsed chariot, to enjoy
      Her love among the stars. For us, vain dreaming,
      False hopes. The gods hate Troy.

      Enter MENELAUS.

MENELAUS.

Even the sun shines brighter today,   860
This most glorious of days when I shall finally
Get my hands on that wife of mine, Helen.
Yes, I am the man, Menelaus,
Who for ten years have endured this terrible war –
Together with the Greek army. But it wasn't only
For my wife's sake that I came to Troy.
People say that, I know. My real motive
Was to get my hands on the man who stole
My wife, violated the sanctity
Of my much loved home, treacherously
Deceived me, his host, and thumbed his nose
At every known principle of hospitality!
Well. I've certainly made him pay for that –
With the gods' help of course – him,
And all his people – the Greeks have butchered
The lot, and turned his great city
Into a wilderness. But certainly, too,
I have come to fetch the Spartan woman –
It gives me no pleasure to speak her name –   870
The woman who was my wife. She's been counted
Into this temporary prison with the rest
Of the Trojan women. The Greek soldiers,
Whose blood and guts have been tested and spent
In so many battles to get her back
Have handed her over to me, to kill her
Here on the spot – unless I decide
To take her back to our Argive homeland.
That's up to me. In fact, I've decided
To pass up the opportunity of killing Helen
Here in Troy, and to row her home
To Greece, where she will be handed over
To the relatives of all those who died at Troy
To be executed in payment for their blood.
Get in there, you guards, into that building,   880
And bring her out here, drag her out
By the hair, sticky with dead men's blood,
The murderess! And as soon as the wind's

In the right quarter, we'll ship her off to Greece.

HECUBA.

Oh Zeus, you who at the same time
Support the earth like a great pillar
And sit throned upon it, unknown, unknowable,
Whether we call you a force of nature
Or an image in the mind of man, hear
The prayer I offer, as mysteriously, unheard,
You lead men's footsteps in the paths of Justice!

MENELAUS.

That's a new way to pray to the gods!

HECUBA.

890   If you mean to kill your wife, Menelaus,
You'll have my support. But don't see her,
Don't risk becoming a slave
Of your lust again. With one look
She makes men's eyes her prisoners, she sacks
Whole cities, burns houses to the ground
With that bewitching smile! I know her,
And so do you, everyone who's met her
And suffered for it knows her well enough!

Enter HELEN, *guarded.*

HELEN.

Menelaus . . . if this is just the start
I'm terrified of what may come next . . . ! Your guards
Have dragged me out here in front of the building
With such violence and contempt . . . You hate me, I know.
I'm almost sure you do. But this one question
I must ask you nevertheless. What have the Greeks
Decided – what have you decided –
900   To do with me? Am I to live or die?

MENELAUS.

Nothing definite was decided. But the army unanimously
Gave you to me, your wronged husband, to kill you.

HELEN.

Can I speak in my own defence, and show
How unjust it would be to kill me – if you do?

MENELAUS.

I've come for an execution, not an argument.

HECUBA.

Hear her Menelaus, let her speak,
Don't let her die without a word
In her own defence! And then let me
Make the case against her! What do you know
Of the havoc she has caused in Troy? Nothing.
When I've had my say, read the whole indictment,
There'll be no room for any doubt that she's guilty.   910

MENELAUS.

You're asking a favour, and that will take time.
But if she wants to speak, that can be allowed.
It's for your sake, be quite clear, that I allow it, not hers.

HELEN.

It probably doesn't matter if I speak well
Or badly, if you've already decided
Against me. You won't even bother to answer.
But if your accusations against me
Are what I think they will be, I shall answer
Your arguments with arguments of my own.
First of all, this woman, Hecuba,
She gave birth to all the trouble by giving birth   920
To Paris. Secondly, *he* destroyed Troy,
Priam did, the old King, and he destroyed me too,
When he failed to strangle his brat at birth,
Paris Alexander, seeing in him, as he did,
An image of that firebrand that would burn Troy.
And then what happened? Listen, and I'll tell you.
Paris had three goddesses in one harness,
And sat in judgement on their beauty. Pallas
Offered him the leadership
Of a Trojan expeditionary force
That would take out the whole of Greece! Hera
Promised that if he gave her the prize
He would become the master of Europe
And the whole of Asia. But Aphrodite
Simply and rapturously described how beautiful

I was, promised him he should have me
930   If he chose her as the most beautiful
Of the three goddesses. Think carefully
About what happened next. Aphrodite won the prize,
And think what a blessing my marriage to Paris
Was to Greece! You are not under the heel
Of a barbarian conqueror, not defeated in battle,
No totalitarian dictator has you at his mercy.
But Hellas' good fortune was my ruin,
Exported, I was, sold off abroad,
My exceptional beauty was a saleable asset
For Greece! And now all I get is vulgar abuse
Instead of the respect and honour I deserve!
You will say, no doubt, that I have ignored
The main point, the reason why
I ran away from your home in secret.
940   He came, call him Paris, or Alexander,
Whichever of his names you like, that genius
Of destruction Hecuba gave birth to, and with him
Came a goddess, well, not exactly a weakling
As goddesses go . . . And you, spineless idiot,
You chose that moment of all moments
To leave your home and take ship for Crete!
Are you beginning to understand? The next question
Is the crucial one, and I ask it of myself,
Not you. What, if anything at all,
Was I thinking of when I tamely followed
This foreigner, whom I hardly knew,
Betraying my country, and my home, and my family
In the process? Ask the goddess, not me,
Punish her, punish the destructive power
Of love; and in doing so, proclaim yourself
Superior to Zeus, who is the master
Of all the gods, but the slave of that one,
Aphrodite! That being the case,
950   What can you honestly do but forgive me?
There is, I suppose, one further accusation
You might make against me. Once Paris was dead
And in his grave, since my marriage was no longer

The direct responsibility of the goddess, I should
Have left his house and made my escape
To the Greek ships. God knows, I wanted to,
And God knows how I tried! Ask the guard commanders
At the great tower posterns, ask the sentries
On the walls, ask them how many times
They caught me lowering my clumsy body
In secret from the battlements of Troy,
Or shinning down ropes to reach the ground!
But my new husband Deiphobus – he's dead too –
Took me by force, made me be his wife!
All the Trojans were against it. Well then.   960
Husband. Can you still think it right to kill me?
Could you do such a thing with any justice?
I had no choice. I was raped, not married.
My life in Troy was the most abject slavery,
Nothing glorious about it. And I have destroyed them.
The gods have acted. Will you oppose them?
Only a fool would dare to do that.

CHORUS.

Speak up for your children now, dear Queen,
Speak for your country! Show her arguments for what they
                                                                  are,
Fluent, but wicked. She's a dangerous woman!

HECUBA.

First I shall speak for the goddesses, and expose
This woman's slanders for the rubbish they are!   970
The gods are not fools. Hera and the virgin
Pallas would never have perpetrated
Such acts of brainless stupidity. Would Hera
Ever sell her own city of Argos
To the barbarians? Or could Pallas conceivably
Allow Athens to come under foreign domination
Simply for the sake of a game? If they went
To Mount Ida at all, for mere childish amusement,
And the vanity of beautiful women!
Why should Hera so suddenly fall victim
To an insatiable craving to be thought beautiful?

To get a more aristocratic husband
For herself than Zeus? And is Athene
Now on the lookout for a husband among the gods?
980   Her hatred of marriage is well known, she pleaded
With her father for eternal virginity,
And he granted it. Don't attempt to disguise
Your own wickedness by accusing the Immortals
Of such stupidity. No sensible person
Will be taken in. And Aphrodite herself,
You say – this is ludicrous, laughable –
Came with my son to Menelaus' house!
Is it likely? She could have stayed at home
On Olympus, and taken you, the Royal Palace
At Amyclae, the whole lot, to Ilium,
With the merest gesture, if she'd wanted to.
But that wasn't it! My son had the sort
Of good looks women run mad for,
You were wet with lust the moment you saw him!
That was your Aphrodite! And doesn't everyone
Dignify their appetite and stupidity
990   By invoking the goddess' name, blaming her?
Sensuality and senselessness have more in common
Than a first syllable. The moment you saw him
In his exotic oriental dress
And dripping with gold, you lost your head
Completely. Life in Sparta was austere
By comparison; but once Sparta was behind you
You saw yourself drowning in an ever flowing river
Of Phrygian gold, submerging the whole city
Under a tidal wave of riotous expense!
They were too bleak a stage for you, the bare
Rooms of Menelaus' palace, to overplay
Your fantasies of luxury and indulgence!
And then, my son, you say, dragged you off
By force, that's your version of the story!
Which one of the Spartans saw this happen?
Were there no witnesses? How loudly did you scream?
1000   Your brother Castor was a young man, still alive,
Still living there with his twin, neither of them

Had yet been transformed into heavenly bodies
And taken their places among the stars.
And when you arrived in Troy, with the Greek army
Hot on your heels, and the battles began,
If news reached you that this man's divisions
Had fought a successful engagement, O Menelaus,
No praise was too good for him, so that my son
Ran mad with jealousy and despair
That his rival in love had the upper hand.
But if the Trojans won the day, Menelaus,
Pooh, what was he, he was nothing!
Yes, you always kept a very beady eye
On the main chance, you would make sure
You were on the winning side! Loyalty, duty,
Love? Not worth that much to you, any of it!
And as for this story of yours, how desperate   1010
You were to escape, how you lowered yourself
By rope from the city walls, as if we
Kept you here against your will –
Well, how many times, may I ask, were you caught
In the act of hanging yourself, or sharpening
A knife to cut your own throat, things
Any woman of breeding or nobility
Would be expected at least to attempt, if she were truly
Grieving for her former husband? Not you.
I've lost count of the times I said to you,
'Listen, Daughter, you should get out of here.
My son can find other women
Easily enough. I'll help you to escape
In secret, I'll arrange an escort for you
To the Greek ships, and so we'll make an end
Of this pointless slaughter of Greeks and Trojans.'
But that was not at all the kind of thing
You had in mind. In Alexander's palace
Your most arrogant whim could be indulged,   1020
You loved nothing better than seeing Asiatics
Prostrating themselves at your feet! And how
That mattered to you, how important it made you feel!
And even now, you dare to parade yourself

Like this, wearing make-up, your hair brushed,
With your best dress on, brazenly confronting
Your husband in the open air
Under the eye of heaven! You're worthless.
Respectable women spit at you in contempt.
If you had any decency in you at all
You would have come here on your knees in rags,
Shaven headed, and shivering with fear,
Prepared to humiliate yourself
With every kind of self abasement and shame
For the wicked things you have done. Menelaus,
You can see what I'm getting at. My arguments
All point the same way. Consummate

1030   The Greek victory by killing your wife!
Death is what she deserves. And other women
Will learn from her example that wives who betray
Their husbands must expect to die for it.

CHORUS.

Menelaus, punish your wife in a way
Worthy of the traditions of your family. Rescue
The reputation of Greek womanhood by the nobility of your
                          revenge!

MENELAUS.

Your conclusions are exactly the same as my own,
That this woman left my house of her own free will
To go to bed with a foreigner.
To drag in Aphrodite is a mere smokescreen
Of pretentious self importance! Take her away.
Let her face death in the stoning pit.

1040   You can atone for the ten year suffering of the Greeks
With an hour of dying: or however long it takes.
That'll teach you what it costs to humiliate me.

HELEN.

I beg you on my knees, I implore you,
Don't kill because the gods are diseased!

HECUBA.

Remember all your friends who are dead, murdered
By this woman! On my knees, I beg you, remember!

MENELAUS.

    All right old woman, that'll do! I'm not listening
    To her. I'm speaking to my staff . . . Take her
    To where the ships are moored. We're sending her back
                                home.

HECUBA.

    Don't travel in the same ship with her!

MENELAUS.

    Why? Has she put on weight? Will she sink it?   1050

HECUBA.

    Once a lover, always besotted.

MENELAUS.

    No. A sensible man loves someone worthy of his love.
    However, I shall do as you say. We won't
    Go on board the same ship. A reasonable precaution.
    When we arrive in Argos she will be punished
    As she deserves. She's a wicked woman,
    And she will endure a terrible death
    That will be a warning to all women in the future
    To be chaste and moral in their behaviour.
    That's by no means an easy lesson to teach,
    But the manner of her death will terrify
    The most frivolous of females, or others who might be
                               tempted
    To be even more degraded than she is.

Exeunt HELEN, MENELAUS *and guards.*

CHORUS.

    O Zeus, our eyes are open now!   1060
    You have betrayed us to the Greeks – the great
    Temple of Ilium, the flames that glow
    Eternally on the altar of offerings, the sweet
    Pillars of myrrh smoke that rise to heaven,
    The incense thick in the air, even
    The sanctuary of Pergamon, the sacred mountain
    Of Ida, where the melted snow leaps
    In torrents down the ivy covered slopes,
    And first light flushes the eastern crest of dawn's
                          handmaiden.   1070

The beauty of ritual is destroyed, all the sacrifices
Are over, no more hushed singing
Of sacred psalms, watch night services,
Vigils from first dark till dawn, no carrying
Of images cast in gold to the festivals
Of the twelve full moons of Troy. A shadow falls
Like ice in my heart. Do you care, on your radiant throne
In the heavens, do you even remember, King of gods,
That we exist, while the very air explodes
1080   Around us, and fire reduces our city to ashes and stone?

Oh my love, my husband, you are dead!
You are out there somewhere – unwashed, unburied
Your poor ghost wanders aimlessly in the dark.
And ships will carry me over the sea,
Their fast oars beating like wings, to the city
Of the horse breeders, Argos, whose great stone walls are
                                      the work
Of the Cyclopes, and seem to touch the sky.
But our children, a great crowd of them, weep and moan
Down by the gates, clinging desperately to their mothers,
1090   all their pain,
Screaming and tears to no avail.
'Mother,' they sob, 'the Greeks will haul
Me away to their black ships, I shall be all
Alone, and the sea-going oars
Will sweep me across to sacred Salamis,
Or to where between two seas the Acropolis
Of Corinth guards Pelops' doors!'

1100   I have one wish: that when Menelaus' ship
Is in the open sea, with a terrifying thunderclap
From the hand of Zeus it will be struck by lightning
Amidships, right between the oars,
And far out in the Aegean! I shall be in tears
Then, exiled from Troy, dehumanised, reduced to a thing
That slaves for the Greeks: while Helen peers
Like a self-regarding schoolgirl in her mirrors of gold
Admiring her good looks. My wish for her's soon told.
Dear gods, let her never come safe home

To Sparta, never repossess that bedroom   1110
In her own house and hearth, never come
Again to the village of Pitana, as once she could,
Nor re-enter Athene's temple with the great bronze door,
This woman whose promiscuity shamed Greece, and
                                        stained the pure
Waters of Simois with blood.

No, no, no more agony!
Our land is under the whip, the next
Stroke falls while we still bleed from the last.
Yes, yes, you may weep, women of Troy! But the worst
Is still to come. They are bringing Astyanax' body,
                                        cast   1120
Like a stone by the Greeks from the towers of Troy.

Enter TALTHYBIUS *and guards with* ASTYANAX' *body,
carried in* HECTOR's *battle shield.*

TALTHYBIUS.
    Hecuba . . . there's only one ship
    Of Neoptolemus' squadron still here. The crew
    Are currently loading his share of the booty
    Before sailing for Phthia. Neoptolemus himself
    Has already set sail, having heard bad news
    From home – his grandfather Peleus, apparently,
    Has been the victim of a military coup,
    Organised by Acastus, the son of Pelias,
    And has had to flee the country. Time
    Is of the essence, so he left at once,
    Taking Andromache with him, whose heartbroken   1130
    Tears as she left her native land,
    And grief-stricken outbursts over the tomb
    Of Hector, brought tears to my eyes too.
    She begged the Prince that you should be allowed
    To bury the body, the son of your son Hector,
    Who gave up his life, as ordered, thrown down
    From the walls of Troy. She begged too, that this shield
    With its bronze back, which has terrified
    The Greeks so many times in the hands
    Of the boy's father, when he advanced protecting

The whole of his body behind it, should not
Be sent across the sea to Peleus' house,
Nor stand as a mute reminder in the same chamber
1140 Where the boy's mother, Andromache, to her grief,
Must give herself a second time as a bride,
But be used instead of a coffin and cairn
Of stones, and that the boy should be buried
Lying beneath it. She asked me to make sure
That the body came into your hands, so that you
Could shroud it with some of your own clothes
And garland it with flowers – insofar as you can
In your present difficult circumstances.
She, because of her master's great haste,
Is robbed of the opportunity of burying her child
Herself, and is already gone. We, let me emphasise,
As soon as you have laid out the body,
Buried him, and heaped up the earth on his grave,
Must step the mast, make sail, and away.
So you must do what you have to do
1150 As quickly as possible. One thing
I have done for you. As we came back
Across the Scamander, I took the opportunity
To wash the body, and wipe away
The dirt and blood from his wounds. Well then . . .
I shall now make it my business to dig
A grave for the boy, so that my work will end
As quickly as yours must; and then, with the greatest
Possible expedition, we can all go home.

HECUBA.

Oh, the great arc of Hector's shield! Here,
Put it on the ground . . . My eyes
Are stabbed to the brain. I never dreamed
They would see such a sight. O you Greeks,
You are so proud of yourselves as fighting men
And thinkers! Are you proud of this too?
Why him? Were you so frightened of a child
You had to invent this unheard of savagery?
1160 Did you think he would rebuild fallen Troy

From this rubble on his own? You're nothing,
You're worth nothing, we could all see that
When Hector was riding his good fortune,
With ten thousand men fighting at his side,
Destroying you beneath his spear. But now,
When the city is taken, and every Trojan
Fighting man lies dead, you have become terrified
Of a little child. What cowards you are,
How I despise blind panic,
Unreasoning terror in rational men!
My little darling . . . what a wretched, meaningless death
Has been meted out to you! If you had died
On your feet, defending your city,
In the full glory of your young manhood,
Having tasted the pleasures of marriage,   1170
One of the god-Kings of Troy, everyone
Would have called you a happy man – if
Any of these things is worth the name
Of happiness. But though your child's soul
May have glimpsed or sensed the glories
You were born to, they have slipped from your grasp.
Before you were old enough to enjoy them.
My poor little boy, how dreadfully your head
Has been shaved by the walls of your own city,
Built by the prophetic god Apollo
For your ancestors. These beautiful curls
Your mother so much loved to stroke and kiss
And bury her face in, torn out, shorn to stubble.
The blood's still oozing from the broken bones
Laughing at us in its mockery of life . . .
No . . . no more of that. It degrades the decency
Of speech to put such things into words . . .
Sweet little hands, the image of your father's,
So limp and lifeless now, mere appendages
Flopping at the end of your arms. And your lips,   1180
So delicious in all their childish chattering,
And now so cold and dead! What lies you told me
When you snuggled down among my bedclothes.
'Grandmother,' you used to say, 'I shall cut

The biggest curl you ever saw from my head
For you when you are dead, and I'll bring
All my friends to your tomb, to make speeches
And sing songs of farewell.' But now,
That promise will never be kept. And I
An old woman, with her city destroyed
And all her children dead, must bury you,
So much younger than I am, such a tender corpse.
My dear little sweetheart, what use were all
Those cuddles I gave you, the times I nursed you,
Fed you, and got you off to sleep,
All my love wasted when it comes to this,
With you dead in my arms. What memorial verses
Would a poet write to be carved on your tombstone?
1190   'This child was murdered by the Greeks
Because they were afraid of him!' May all Hellas
Forever be ashamed of such an epitaph!
Well, little grandson, everything
You should have inherited from your father you have lost,
Except this shield with its curved bronze back,
And that, my dear, you will keep forever
As it covers you in the earth. Women,
Do you see? This is the shield that protected
Hector's magnificent arm! He for sure
Was this shield's best protector, and now he is dead.
Look, you can clearly see the imprint
Of his powerful hand on the grip, and here
On the brass facing and the smooth rim
You can see how his beard has burnished it
As he held it up to his chin, and where
The sweat, pouring down from his forehead and temples
In so many hot fought afternoons of battle
Has left its dark stain. Come now, my women,
See what you can find, some robe, if you can,
1200   Or some flowers somewhere, to dress his poor body
For burial. It's little enough, child,
We can give you, in this time of disaster.
But what we can find, you shall have. Anyone
Born mortal and living in this world, who thinks

Himself prosperous and secure, is a fool.
Historical necessity, or whatever else you call
The force that governs our lives, what else is it
But a madman dancing, leaping one way then the next
Without pattern or meaning? What's certain
Is that luck always runs out, and that no happy man
Ever stays happy or lucky for long.

CHORUS.

Look Hecuba, we found these things among the ruins.
They'll do to prepare the body for burial.

HECUBA.

Dear child, it's not after some victory
At horse racing with fellows your own age,
Or archery, that I, your father's mother,
Award you these meagre prizes. We Trojans   1210
Esteem such achievements, and honour them as they
                                                    deserve.
These poor things are the only remnants
Of the legendary wealth of Troy, your inheritance,
Of which Helen, whom all the gods hate,
Has robbed you. And more than that, she has taken
Your life, and utterly destroyed your family.

CHORUS.

Let your tears flow!
My heart is breaking, weep and sing
For the dead child who was born to be King!

HECUBA.

This magnificent robe, the height of Trojan fashion!
You should have worn it at your wedding
To the most aristocratic Princess of Asia.
Now I can only use it as a shroud
Or winding sheet to wrap round your body.   1220
And for you, great shield, who protected Hector
Like a mother, and gave birth to victories
Beyond number, a garland of flowers.
You are not dead, nor will ever be,
Though you lie with the dead in the earth: an honour

Greater than the Greeks can pay to the armour
Of that black-hearted politician, Odysseus!

CHORUS.
  Howl then, howl!
  Now, if ever, tear the tears from your breast
  As the earth receives this child to rest.
  Mother, you must share our pain.

HECUBA.

                    Howl . . .

CHORUS.
  Lead our song for the dead.

HECUBA.

1230   For grief!

CHORUS.
  Who can forget these sufferings? Time will bring no relief.

HECUBA.
  With these strips of linen, as if I could heal them
  Let me bind up your wounds. The mere shadow of a doctor
  Without the substance. My fingers are skilful
  But have no art to cure. Your father's hand
  Must care for you now, among the dead.

CHORUS.
  Beat your temples, tear out your hair
  Let your nails rake your face like a bank of oars.

HECUBA.
  My daughters, listen, women of Troy . . .

CHORUS.
  We're still here. Say what you want to say.

HECUBA.
1240 Everything I have done in my life has meant nothing
  To the vindictive gods – and Troy, of all cities,
  They have persecuted with a particular hatred.
  All our sacrifices, all our offerings
  Have been quite worthless, a waste of time.
  And yet . . . if the god had not decided
  To make the greatest suffer most

And trample us all in the mud, what nonentities
We would all have been! No one would ever
Have heard of us, no songs would have been written
In memory of our suffering, nor would the poets
A hundred generations hence have taken us
As their great theme. So take up the body,
And let us bring it to its dishonoured grave.
We have given it all we can of the flowers
And offerings customary for the dead –
And what difference does it make to them
If they are buried in luxury, loaded with gifts.
None at all, I think. Funerals are for the living,
An empty show to impress their friends.   1250

The body of ASTYANAX *is removed.*

CHORUS.
  Weep and sing
  For your suffering mother, who teased out the cloth
  Of your life with such care, all torn and rumpled in death.
  And for the child, a hero's son, no family could be greater
  Than his, born to be King.
  His terrible death men will remember with horror.
  But look. What are they doing?
  There are men with torches, will they destroy
  Even these ruins? On Ilium's surviving towers
  In many hands the bud of flame flowers.
  What more can they do to Troy?

TALTHYBIUS.
  All company commanders with orders   1260
  To fire the city, there's no need to wait
  Any longer, till your torches burn out
  In your hands. Burn everything down!
  When we have reduced the whole lot to ashes
  Then we can celebrate, leave Troy, and go home!
  My other orders concern you women.
  As soon as you hear the sound of the trumpet
  Follow these officers along that path.
  They will lead you to the Greek ships.
  You, old woman, you're the unluckiest

Of the lot. You must go too, with these
1270   Officers of Odysseus' regiment. You must leave
Your old home. You're designated one of his slaves.

HECUBA.

So this is how it ends. My crown of pain,
All my sufferings, each new loss
Worse than the last, till it comes to this:
To leave my homeland, to leave my city,
To watch them burning it to the ground.
Come on then, old worn out feet,
Make one last effort, so that I can say
My last goodbyes to my poor city
In its death agony . . .
Troy! While you lived, you were the greatest
And most glorious of all the cities of Asia.
Now they are destroying even your name.
They are burning you to the ground, and taking us
1280   Into exile to be slaves. O, you gods!
But why bother to call on them? We called before,
And they didn't hear us. They ignored our prayers.
Well then. Why not run into the flames?
What could be better for me, the Queen
Of this burning city, than to die in its embrace
And make its funeral pyre my own!

TALTHYBIUS.

Poor woman. You've suffered so much
It's unbalanced you, like an ecstasy of pain.
Hang on to her! You need not treat her with kid gloves!
She belongs to Odysseus now, and your orders
Are to deliver her personally into his hands.

HECUBA.

Howl! Howl! Howl!
Son of Cronos, god of Troy,
Father of our fatherland, do you see?
1290   Dardanus' children don't deserve such a fall!

CHORUS.

He sees, and does nothing. Troy, our beautiful city,
No longer exists. They are burning, burning it all.

HECUBA.
Howl! Howl! Howl!
Troy is burning, every house is in flames
Even the citadel, walls and domes,
The hungry flames are consuming it all!

CHORUS.
The black wing of heaven shadows the dying houses
Of the murdered Trojans. Smoke is their funeral pall.   1300

HECUBA.
My beloved city, my children's nurse.

CHORUS.
Weep louder, weep long.

HECUBA.
My children, do you hear your mother's voice?

CHORUS.
Cry to the dead. Can they hear your song?

HECUBA.
Let me kneel, lay my old legs on the ground,
And my old woman's hands, let them beat the earth!

CHORUS.
Let me kneel beside you, let my voice sound
In the dark halls of Hades, the Kingdom of Death!
Husband, can you hear me underground?

HECUBA.
Like loot they are stealing us.   1310

CHORUS.
                    Let the dead hear our pain.

HECUBA.
To live in their slave huts, to be a slave.

CHORUS.
Home gone, country gone.

HECUBA.
Priam, you are dead, but you have no grave,
No friend to weep or keen,
Can you hear my anguished moan?

CHORUS.
He hears nothing. The black veil of death
Has darkened his sacred eyes with the desecration of earth.

HECUBA.
My beloved country, temples of the gods . . .

CHORUS.
Weep louder, weep long.

HECUBA.
The fire consumes, and the spear invades.

CHORUS.
Soon anonymous earth, like a forgotten song.

HECUBA.
1320   A cloud of dust darkens the sky
Like a shadowy wing, blots out my old home.

CHORUS.
Soon no one will remember this city,
Everything is dying, even the name:
There is no place on earth called Troy.

HECUBA.
Do you hear that sound?

CHORUS.
                        Troy has fallen!

HECUBA.
It's like an earthquake. Everything's shaking!

CHORUS.
The city sinks, we all drown!

HECUBA.
Into the abyss. My legs are trembling,
But I won't fall. Old limbs, strengthen
1330   Yourselves. Your slavery is beginning.

CHORUS.
Troy is finished. We must turn our weary feet
To the harbour. The oars are waiting. March down to the
                                        Achaean fleet!

Exeunt HECUBA, TALTHYBIUS *and* CHORUS.

IPHIGENIA AT AULIS

translated by Don Taylor

Characters

AGAMEMNON, Commander-in-Chief of the Greek army
OLD MAN, servant of Agamemnon
MENELAUS, brother of Agamemnon, husband of Helen
CLYTEMNESTRA, wife of Agamemnon
IPHIGENIA, their daughter
ACHILLES, a Greek hero
FIRST MESSENGER, from the guard party bringing
Clytemnestra and Iphigenia to Aulis
SECOND MESSENGER, from the sacrifice
CHORUS of women from Chalcis
SECONDARY CHORUS of soldiers
PRIESTS and PRIESTESSES, ATTENDANTS,
ORESTES' NURSE, ARMOUR BEARERS

Before AGAMEMNON's *tent in the Greek camp at Aulis. Enter* AGAMEMNON *with a letter.*

AGAMEMNON.
Old man. Come out, in front of the hut.
Stand here.

Enter the OLD MAN.

OLD MAN.
        I'm coming. Another bright idea,
King Agamemnon, eh?

AGAMEMNON.
              Hurry!

OLD MAN.
                I'm hurrying.
I don't sleep much. Too old for that.
Old age keeps your eyes sharp as a sentry.

AGAMEMNON.
What star's that? Like a ship crossing the night sky.

OLD MAN.
That's Sirius. Next to the seven Pleiades:
Still rising there, in the mid heaven.

AGAMEMNON.
No birdsong. Even the sound of the sea
Is muffled. But the lack of wind: that silence   10
Holds back more than the waves in the Straits of Euripus.

OLD MAN.
But why come out of your hut, King Agamemnon,
Just to pace up and down the same
Few steps? All quiet at Aulis tonight.
Not a sound from the guard towers on the walls.
Let's go back in.

AGAMEMNON.
           Old friend, I envy you.
I envy anyone who can get through life
Unnoticed, avoiding danger, and without fame.
Famous men, great leaders. I don't envy them at all.

OLD MAN.

20   But they get all the glory, sir. They win life's prizes.

AGAMEMNON.

Yes, you say so. But glory is dangerous.
And honour slippery;
You have it, and it's gone. Ambition for leadership
Is an addiction, thrilling, but painful in the end.
If the gods' wishes and a man's will conflict
His life will be smashed.
And men's conflicting demands shred you like a grater.

OLD MAN.

I don't like to hear this sort of talk
From a great King, Lord Agamemnon.

30   Atreus fathered you
Not just for the pleasures of Kingship
And a life of unbroken good luck. Pain
As well as celebration you must expect.
You're a man, born mortal. And the gods
Regardless of whether you like it or not
Will have their way.
You light your lamp, it flares up, and spreads
Enough light for you to write a letter.
You're still holding it in your hand. You write
A bit, then cross it out, then write again,
And cross it out again,
Seal it up, and immediately unseal it,
Even throw it on the ground: all the time

40   Weeping real tears.
You looked so desperate, you seemed half mad
With some trouble or other. Is it bad news
That causes so much grief? You can tell me, my Lord.
I'm loyal and trustworthy. I came with your wife,
Sent with her from Tyndareus I was,
Part of the dowry!

AGAMEMNON.

Thestius' daughter, Leda, bore three daughters:
50   Phoebe, Clytemnestra – who became my wife –

And Helen. All the leading young men of Greece
Were mad for Helen, and came as suitors,
Each one threatening his rivals with murder
And mayhem, if he didn't get the girl.
Tyndareus, their father, was baffled, how, either
In giving or refusing her, to make the best of a bad job.
But then an idea struck him: a pact,
That all the suitors should consent to, shaking hands,
And confirmed with the usual religious ceremonies –
Burned offerings, the pouring of wine, etcetera –
Which would bind every one of them, by oath,   60
To defend and support whichever man
Won the daughter of Tyndareus as his wife,
In the event that anyone should abduct her
From her husband's bed. Whoever he was,
Greek or barbarian, they would mount a fully armed
Expeditionary force against him, and destroy
His city. When they'd committed themselves,
And old Tyndareus, being a crafty fellow,
Had sewn them up neatly with his logic,
He smartly allowed his daughter to let
The breath of the goddess of love blow her
Towards whichever one of the suitors she chose.   70
And she chose . . . God help us, *him*, of all people . . .
Menelaus. Not long after that, from Troy,
The principal city of Phrygia, a young fellow
By the name of Paris – the very same man,
According to the story rife among the Greeks,
Who judged between three goddesses, and chose beauty
Before wisdom and power – turned up in Sparta.
The splendour of his dress was barbaric,
A vulgar ostentation of gold and jewels,
Cloth of gold, flowered silk, and gems
In the shape of flowers, glittering, shining . . .
Helen was dazed with lust for him
And he for her. He picked his moment –
Menelaus was out of the country – and dragged her
Off to his byres and bartons and pigsties.
On Mount Ida. Menelaus raved like a madman

Through all the cities of Greece, invoking
Tyndareus' old treaty they had all set their hands to,
Claiming, indeed demanding they must all
Stand by their guarantees and launch
A punitive expedition, to sack Troy!
80   So all the Greeks sprang out of their chariots,
Took down spears, and shields, and body armour from their
                                                                    walls,

And came here, to this natural harbour of Aulis,
Opposite the narrows, with their ships,
Their heavy armour, thousands of horse,
And their decorated battle chariots. They gave
Supreme command to me, for Menelaus' sake,
Because I am his brother. And I swear to God,
I wish any other man had been given that honour
Rather than me. And now we are all here,
Mustered at Aulis, this vast army,
There's not a breath of wind, we all wait,
Unable to get even one ship under way.
We have waited, and waited, and we began to despair;
Till the Priest Calchas spoke: and he said . . .
90   That we must offer my daughter, my child, Iphigenia,
As a sacrifice to the goddess of this place, Artemis,
Who has her sanctuary here. And then, only then
The wind would change, we could put to sea,
Sail across to Phrygia, and sack Troy.
When I heard this, I immediately told Talthybius,
Our Communications and Propaganda Officer,
To announce the disbandment of the whole army,
Because I couldn't – not conceivably,
Ever be so brutal as to kill my own child . . .
When he heard this, my brother begged me,
He wheedled and exerted every argument
And persuasion he could think of, till finally
He forced me to agree to the damnable business.
I wrote a letter, folded it, and folded it again,
And sent it to my wife. It told her to send
100   Our daughter here, to be married to Achilles.
I made a great fuss of him, told her how heroic

He was, praised him to the skies, and said
He absolutely refused to sail with us
Unless a bride should be sent from our family
To return with him to his house at Phthia.
I was sure this pack of lies about our daughter's marriage
Would be convincing enough to persuade my wife.
Of all the Greeks, only the Priest Calchas,
Odysseus, and Menelaus, and myself
Know about this . . . I did that . . . And I was wrong!
So in this new letter I have changed my decision,
Back to what I decided in the first place.
That's what I was doing, writing and rewriting,
Sealing and unsealing in my hut in the dark.   110
Now take it, go on, now, get to Argos
Fast. No, wait, I'd better let you
Into the secret sealed up in there
Word for word. You're a good fellow,
You've been loyal to my wife and to me for years.

OLD MAN.

Yes, you should tell me, so that what I say
Won't conflict with what's written in the letter.

AGAMEMNON.

'Further to my last letter, Daughter of Leda,
These new instructions: do *not* send,
Repeat, *not* send, your daughter here
To this peaceful harbour of Aulis
On the Gulf of Euboea.   120
It seems we must celebrate our daughter's marriage
At some other, future time.'

OLD MAN.

But if Achilles is cheated of his bride,
He'll explode with anger, surely?
His fury towards you and your wife will be terrifying.
You surely don't intend that to happen?

AGAMEMNON.

No, no, I'm merely using his name,
He's not required to do anything. In fact
He knows nothing at all of the matter, he's party

130   To none of our plans, least of all the scheme
      Of his own pretended marriage to my daughter.

OLD MAN.
      It's clever, Lord Agamemnon, but dangerous, to pretend
      You're bringing her to marry the son of an immortal,
      When really, she'll be given to the Greeks, to be
                                          butchered . . .

AGAMEMNON.
      Don't say that . . . ! It drives me mad to hear it.
      I feel as if my head's breaking in pieces . . .
      Get moving, superannuated fool. Forget your legs are old,
      Run like a boy!

OLD MAN.

140   As fast as I can, my Lord.

AGAMEMNON.
      Make sure you don't sit down by that spring in the forest
      And fall asleep.

OLD MAN.

                       As if I would sir, really!

AGAMEMNON.
      When you come to the place where the road forks,
      Look sharply in both directions, and make sure
      No carriage slips past you while you are looking
      The other way, and brings her here,
      To where the whole Greek fleet is anchored.

OLD MAN.
      I'll take care of that sir.

AGAMEMNON.
                       Even if you meet her
150   At the very gates, with her guards and outriders,
      Stop them, grab the reins yourself, and drive her
      Straight back inside the city walls –
      They're so massive, the one-eyed giants built them,
      So the legend says, when Argos was founded.

OLD MAN.

Just a minute though sir . . . why should your wife
And daughter believe me, when I tell them all this?

AGAMEMNON.

This is my seal . . . see here, on the letter.
Make sure it's unbroken. Get moving! The sky
Is greying already. The four-horsed chariot
Of the sun is galloping towards the eastern
Horizon, flooding the sea and sky with light.
It's up to you to save me!   160

Exit the OLD MAN.

AGAMEMNON.

No man lives happy to the end of his life
Or avoids his share of bad luck.
We inherit grief merely by being born.

Exit AGAMEMNON.

Enter the CHORUS.

CHORUS.

I have sailed across the narrow seas
Of Euripus, through the fast running tide,
And landed here on the sandy beach
Of Aulis. My home is on the other side
Of the straits, Chalcis, where Arethusa sprays   170
Her fountain of fresh spring water within reach
Of the salt sea itself. I have come to gaze
In wonder upon the Achaean force,
And the forest of seagoing oars that will pull
The slender pine ships, a thousand strong,
By the strength of brave men's arms, the long
Journey to Troy led by the powerful
Red-headed Menelaus,
And noble Agamemnon, the King!
They'll drag her back here, our husbands say,
Helen, whom Aphrodite gave as a prize
To Paris, the Prince who lived as a shepherd.   180
He found her, where the sighing reed beds whispered

By the river Eurotas – as was promised when the goddess
                                                    arose
Glistening from her bath in a fountain of spray,
When Hera and Pallas and she
Competed so bitterly
For his voice on that Judgement Day.
I ran through the sacred grove of trees,
By Artemis' shrine, where they offer fresh blood
From the victims' throats – my cheeks are crimson
With embarrassment, that in such a crowd
We should come to gawp at the Greek armies,
190   Their huge interlinked shields, like a brazen
Wall, the weapons in their armories
Or stacked by their tents, the heavy cavalry,
But most of all, the men! Ajax I saw,
Oileus' son, just sitting there, talking
To the other Ajax, son of Telamon. He was looking
Every inch the part of the superstar
Of Salamis! And nearby,
Protesilaus was playing draughts, and enjoying
The interplay of chance and strategy
With Palamedes, the sea god's grandson! Diomedes too
200   Was working out with the discus, and revelling
In showing off his strength; and strolling
Close by, Meriones, in battle worth two
Normal men, who claims the war god as his paternity.
And Laertes' son is here
From mountainous Ithaca;
And Nireus, isn't he a beauty!

And Achilles I saw, who runs fast as the wind,
Whom Thetis the sea nymph bore,
And was tutored by Chiron, in body and mind:
He was sprinting along the sea shore
With a full armour on his back,
210   Keeping pace for pace with one of the crack
Charioteers, for battle and track,
Eumelos, with a racing four!
And the son of Pheretias spurred on his team

Around the lap marker to win,
And he tickled their flanks with his whip, and the scream
Of the driver himself urged them on.
Their bits and harness were all gold,   220
The yoke horses grey, with manes piebald,
Red-maned the trace horses, but patterned with bold
Black and white, to the fetlock down.
But the son of Peleus, in full pack,
Ran with them, and matched each stride,
While the whirling wheels
And the screaming axle
And the bouncing chariot rail
Raced inches from his side!   230

And I saw an Armada of ships in the bay,
Too many to count, awesome beyond measure.
I couldn't speak, I was dumb with the joy,
A sight for my eyes to feed on and treasure
As a bee feeds on nectar and stores honey.
Massing on the right, their oars keeping time,
The Myrmidons' battle galleys hove to,
Fast movers from Phthia, like a full rhyme
Closing the line. And high above the waters,
Carved on the sterns in gold, I saw in full view   240
Achilles' coat of arms, Poseidon's sea-born daughters!

Keel by keel with them, equal in number,
The fifty ships of Argos stood,
Sthenelus, tough Capaneus' son,
Captained a squadron, and the pride of Talaos' blood,
Mecistes' heir, was supreme commander.
On station beside them rode sixty ships
From Attica, their Admiral
The son of Theseus. For his emblem he keeps
Pallas herself, carved as she flew   250
In her winged four-handed chariot, a symbol
Sure to bring good luck to any Athenian crew.

With my own eyes I saw
Boeotia's naval power,
A fleet of fifty ships, and each one crowned

With a carven figurehead,
While at each stern post stood
Cadmus, with a golden dragon curled around.
260   Leitus – born of a giant, the ancient earth
Herself – commanded,
And Ajax, Oileus' son, led fifty, worth
His fame, assembled
From Phocis and from Locris, sailing on
From their port of embarkation, famous Thronion.

From Argos' Cyclops walls
The son of Atreus calls
Men by the thousand to crew his hundred ships.
With him his friend and brother
Sails as co-commander
So that Greece may take full payment for the lips
270   Sold in marriage to a barbarian, and the hearth
And home destroyed.
And Nestor from Gerenon, loth
To be unemployed
Sails in, ignoring his great age,
With bull-foot Alpheus the river god as his badge.

The King Gouneus captained a line
Of twelve Aeneanian ships, a fine
Flotilla, and alongside them
280   The tribesmen of Elis, whom everyone
In the army calls Epeians: beside them the squadron –
Whose oars, from stem
To stern were painted gleaming white –
Of the Taphians, mirroring the sun's light.
Eurytus led them: and Phyleus' son was there,
Meges, from the Echinean islands, whose rocks all sailors
fear.

Ajax from Salamis held the centre
290   Joining right wing and left together
Manoeuvring his line
Of light fast moving craft to meet
And link his wings with the rest of the fleet
Like closing a chain.

The task force was ready, as if on parade,
Both army and navy. No commando raid
Or foreign battle fleet would dare to face
So vast a navy, and hope for safe return to base.   300

Like a city on the sea, I watched the Greek fleet
Assembling in the bay.
Others may speak of it, but my eyes have seen it.
I will never forget this day!

Enter MENELAUS *with the* OLD MAN. MENELAUS *has*
AGAMEMNON's *letter in his hand.*

OLD MAN.
Menelaus, you dare not, have you no conscience . . . ?

MENELAUS.
Get off! Unquestioning loyalty is as bad.

OLD MAN.
Do you mean that as an insult? I call it praise.

MENELAUS.
Look, if you overstep the mark, you'll be sorry!

OLD MAN.
You had no right to open the letter I was carrying.

MENELAUS.
The letter you were carrying betrays every one of us!

OLD MAN.
You carry on shouting, but give me that letter!

MENELAUS.
I've got it, and I'll keep it!

OLD MAN.

                              I won't let it go!   310

MENELAUS.
I'll bloody your head for you with this stick if you don't.

OLD MAN.
I'll die for my master then, and be famous!

MENELAUS.
Let go! For a batman, you talk too much.

OLD MAN.
> My Lord! This is an outrage! Come out sir!
> This man has torn your letter from my hand
> Agamemnon, by force, quite without conscience.

Enter AGAMEMNON.

AGAMEMNON.
> Hey there . . . !
> What's all this racket, this abuse, at my door?

MENELAUS.
> Listen to me first, this man's a servant!

AGAMEMNON.
> Menelaus, what's this brawling? Let go of that man!

MENELAUS.
320   Pay attention to me then, I'll tell you from the start.

Exit OLD MAN.

AGAMEMNON.
> Atreus was my father. I'll look any man in the eye.

MENELAUS.
> This letter is treasonable, a complete betrayal!

AGAMEMNON.
> I can see it . . . So first of all, give it to me.

MENELAUS.
> Oh no! Not till I've shown it to the army!

AGAMEMNON.
> So. You've broken the seal. It's none of your business.

MENELAUS.
> Unfortunately for you, I know your filthy plan.

AGAMEMNON.
> How did you get hold of it? Have you no shame?

MENELAUS.
> Waiting on the road from Argos – for your daughter.

AGAMEMNON.
> How dare you spy on me! The impudence . . . !

MENELAUS.
> When you have an itch you have to scratch. I'm not your
> > slave!   330

AGAMEMNON.
> It's outrageous to interfere in my family affairs!

MENELAUS.
> You're devious and unreliable, you always have been.

AGAMEMNON.
> Smart talk, excuses for shabby behaviour!

MENELAUS.
> You've no character or resolution,
> You're quite capable of wickedness, and impossible
> To trust, even for your friends! I'm going
> To show you up for what you are – don't
> Turn away like that, it'll be the truth,
> Without any exaggeration – so don't dismiss it
> With a show of anger! You remember, I'm sure,
> When you were so keen to get the supreme command
> Of the Greek task force against Troy,
> And how you wanted it! – There was no pretence
> About that! How very self deprecating
> You were, eager to press the flesh
> With any uniform or suit, doors always open,   340
> A universal welcome; you always granted
> The pleasure of your company
> To anyone, even if they didn't want it,
> As if by sweet talk and glad-handing
> The whole country, you could buy the command
> In the open market. But then,
> When your appointment had been confirmed,
> Suddenly, you were a changed man!
> Friends were no longer friends, overnight.
> No one could get near you, you were always
> Unobtainable, your headquarters' doors
> More often locked than open. A great man,
> A man of genuine nobility
> Who achieves a position of power, does not
> Celebrate his good fortune by cutting

All his friends dead, at the very time
When he's able to do them some good! I saw
The contemptible side of your character
Straight away. But then, when you came here,
350   To Aulis, with the whole Panhellenic
Army trembling at your command,
You became a nonentity, you panicked,
You were struck dumb, or cursed your bad luck
Because there was no wind, and without wind
None of us could get across to Troy!
And the word went round the army, all the Greek
Commanders began to mutter they were wasting
Their time, that we might as well disband
The army, decommission the ships,
Instead of spending time and money at Aulis
For no purpose. You were being called –
Of all damning descriptions – an unlucky General.
You began to see your great dream of leading
A thousand ships to Troy, of darkening
The plain before Priam's city
With division upon division of infantry, disappearing
Before your eyes! You asked my advice
Then, quickly enough. 'What shall I do,
How can we get across, or get out of this trap
Without me losing what I value most,
The glory of command! And then, when Calchas
Came up with a solution, that you should offer
360   Your child to Artemis, as a sacred blood sacrifice,
In return for fair winds and an easy passage,
You were delighted, you jumped at the suggestion,
You willingly offered to murder your daughter;
In fact, of your own volition – none of us
Forced you, you can't say we did – you hurried
Word to your wife to send your child here,
With a rigmarole about her marrying Achilles.
And now, with yet another U-turn,
You've been caught out secretly changing your story
Once again, with another letter. You will never
Be your own daughter's murderer! But you will!

You know what you said. The very air,
The sky above our heads, heard you say it.
Well, it's not surprising I suppose.
Thousands of men have done the same,
Struggled inch by inch up the slippery slope
To power, and then, when they got there,
Slid ignominiously back down to the bottom.
Sometimes it's because the voters are too dim
To understand what they're doing. Other times
They're simply not up to the job. It's Greece   370
I feel sorry for. She intended to act
Honourably. Now she's humiliated,
Made a laughing stock, by a bunch of effeminate
Barbarians, and all because of you
And your little girl. It's always a mistake,
In politics, and in military matters
To appoint a leader simply because
He's brave, and bull-headed. Any man
With a modicum of sense can rule a city.
An army commander needs intelligence, brains!

CHORUS.
It's a terrible thing when angry words, and the threat
Of blows, cause such division between brothers.

AGAMEMNON.
Now I shall have my say. I shall be
Critical, but brief, and stay within
The bounds of decency, without being
Contemptuous to the point of demeaning myself.
You are, after all, my brother. A gentleman   380
Recognises certain norms of behaviour,
He treats other people with courtesy and respect.
What is the point of all this blustering
And eyes bloodshot with fury? Has someone
Wronged you? And if so, what do you expect
Me to do about it? If a faithful wife
Is what you want, I'm afraid I can't help you
There. You let the one you had
Run riot. So am I to pay

For your mistakes, when I am myself
Quite blameless? What gnaws at your
Self esteem isn't my rank,
Or the honours that have been heaped upon me.
To hell with reason, forethought, or any
Kind of decent behaviour, all you want
Is to get that lascivious woman back
In your arms, and into bed. The pleasures
Of a degraded mind are like itself,
Degraded. If I, on the other hand,
Initially made a bad decision
And after coming to my senses
Changed my mind, does that make me mad?
No! You're the mad one. You had the good luck
To lose a wife who was worthless, the gods
Granted you that good fortune. Now
390   You're mad enough to want the bitch back!
All the suitors were half crazed with lust
For her, and like fools, consented to swear
Tyndareus' oath – that most deceiving of goddesses,
Hope, no doubt, leading them on.
It certainly wasn't out of any sense of loyalty
To you! Well then, go and get them
To be your army and do your fighting!
They're ready enough for any madness.
The gods are not lacking in intelligence,
They can tell the difference between genuine vows
And oaths sworn foolishly, or under duress.
I will not kill my children.
You won't get revenge on your worthless wife
At the expense of my sense of justice, leaving me
Years of misery and a guilty conscience
For an unforgivable crime committed
On a child of my own flesh. So there you are.
A few words, brief, and to the point.
You may choose to act like a madman.
400   My business, particularly with my own family,
Will be conducted with decency, and common sense.

CHORUS.

These words completely contradict what you said
Before. But it must be right to spare your child.

MENELAUS.

That leaves me naked, with no friends at all.

AGAMEMNON.

You have friends, if you don't try to destroy them.

MENELAUS.

No one would believe that you are my brother.

AGAMEMNON.

I'm your brother in common sense, not lunacy.

MENELAUS.

A brother should share his brother's agony!

AGAMEMNON.

If you're just, I'll help you. This way you'll destroy me!

MENELAUS.

Greece needs you. Won't you share her agony?   410

AGAMEMNON.

Greece has gone mad. The gods have touched you all!

MENELAUS.

You glory in the power your Field Marshal's baton
Gives you: and you choose to betray me. Very well.
There are other methods; other friends.

A MESSENGER *enters.*

MESSENGER.

                                        Agamemnon!
King of the Greek army! I am one of the escort
Travelling with your daughter to Aulis, the girl
You called Iphigenia when you were at home.
Her mother is with her, your Clytemnestra
In person, and your baby boy,
Orestes. It'll give you particular pleasure
To see him, having been away from home
For so long. We had a tough journey,
And I left the women relaxing by a fresh   420
Spring, and cooling their feet in the pond –

We'd unharnessed the horses and turned them loose
To graze in a nearby field – while I ran
Ahead to tell you what's happened. The army
Knows all about it. You know how fast
Rumour travels. Everyone seems to know
About your daughter's arrival. A big crowd
Has already come out from the camp, trying
To get a look at her. Everyone likes to see
Famous people with the good luck to be born rich
And gossip about them. They're all saying,
430   'What's going on, some marriage, or what?
Or has Agamemnon brought his daughter here
Simply because he's missing her?' I've heard
Some others, though, who say it's a consecration
To Artemis, the Virgin Queen of Aulis,
By way of preparation for marriage.
So who's to be the lucky bridegroom?
If it's true, come on then, we'd better prepare
Baskets of flowers, and floral crowns,
And Lord Menelaus, you must organise the music,
Send for the flutes, and make sure there's plenty
Of dancing, for a day like this, from first dawn
Onwards, should be all happiness for the girl.

AGAMEMNON.
440   Thank you for your news. Go inside for a moment.
If the gods are with us, things will turn out well . . .

Exit the MESSENGER.

AGAMEMNON.
God help me, what can I say
Or do, in a situation like this?
I'm like a slave under the yoke,
Chained and shackled! Bad luck has second-guessed me,
Every move I make is countered, every tactic
Outwitted by a better one! It's better to be born
Nobody, nonentities can cry their eyes out
And blurt out everything to anyone.
For our sort, born in the ruling class,
We must keep our mouths shut, suffer in silence

To protect our position, and our dignity!
The masses are our masters, we their slaves –   450
And that's my situation exactly.
I'm ashamed to cry about it. But I'd be
Ashamed not to cry too. Nothing could be worse
Than being caught in a trap as appalling as this.
And what, in heaven's name, shall I say
To my wife? How can I face her?
How can I look her in the eyes?
What possible expression can my face wear
As it receives her, and welcomes her to Aulis?
I have troubles enough, she has made them
Far worse by coming here uninvited.
And yet it's reasonable enough, natural even,
That she should want to come with her daughter
To see her married, and to give her a mother's
Kisses and endearments on her wedding day.
And then she'll find out soon enough,
If I know her, what mischief I've planned . . .
But the poor maid herself . . . why do I call her   460
That? The god of the dead will take
Her virginity soon enough. It's unendurable
To imagine it . . . She's certain to plead
With me . . . 'Will *you* kill me, Daddy,
You? Then let Death marry you too,
Let him marry everyone you love, the same
As me!' And Orestes will be there,
My little boy. He can't speak yet,
But he'll understand, his unintelligible cries
Will speak far too clearly to my heart . . . Paris,
Priam's son, you are the instigator of all
This pain. Your love for Helen has destroyed me!

CHORUS.
What a moving speech! He's a King, and I'm a woman
From a foreign city, but I sympathise with his grief.   470

MENELAUS.
Brother, let me shake you by the hand.

AGAMEMNON.
   Yes. Why not. You're the winner. I've lost.

MENELAUS.
   Brother, by Pelops, our famous grandfather,
   And by Atreus, who fathered both of us,
   I swear, I'm speaking the plain truth now,
   Direct from the heart, with no hidden motives
   Or any self-interest, but an honest analysis
   Of the facts of the case, and whatever wisdom
   I have learned in my life. When I saw the tears
   In your eyes, I couldn't help pitying you.
   In fact, the tears welled up in my eyes too.
   I retract, unconditionally, all the words and arguments
   I have used against you. I am not your enemy,
   Nor implacable nor destructive in any way
480   Towards you. I stand in your shoes.
   And I beg you not to kill your child
   On my account, or put my interests
   In any way before your own.
   It's not right that you should suffer
   For my pleasure, nor that your child
   Should die, while my children live and enjoy
   The light of day. What is it, after all,
   I want to achieve? A good marriage?
   I could take my pick anywhere in the world,
   If I wanted to. Shall I destroy
   The last person in the world I should injure,
   My own brother, for the sake of the likes
   Of Helen, prefer the wicked woman
   To the good man? I've been thinking
   Stupidly and selfishly, like an adolescent,
   Till watching you, I suddenly had a vision
490   Of what it means to kill a child.
   I was anguished with pity for her, and I realised too
   That we are related, that it's my own niece
   That is to be killed, to preserve my marriage.
   And what has your daughter to do with Helen?
   Nothing in the world. So, disband the army,

Send them all home, away from Aulis.
Anything, Brother, to wipe away these tears
From your cheeks, and mine too, weeping
In sympathy. And . . . even if
You have any secret information
About this sacrifice, which makes it particularly
Acceptable to the gods, let me be quite clear
I want no part of it. My share, the guilt
And all the advantages, I willingly hand over
To you. So you see, I've changed my mind.
All my hostility towards you has gone,   500
Or changed, rather, into something like love.
So it should. You are my brother.
Don't think it cowardice or weakness
That makes me change my mind. Or policy
Masquerading as love. I'm simply determined
To discover the right direction, the best course
For all of us, and follow it through to the end.

CHORUS.

Inspiring words, and worthy Tantalus,
The son of Zeus. Your ancestors would be proud of you.

AGAMEMNON.

What can I say, Menelaus, to thank you
And praise your integrity? Beyond all expectation
You have spoken with an honesty and justice
Worthy of the man I know you to be.
Brothers will always fight, over women
And money, the most lucrative marriage
Or the lion's share of the property,
Or simply because they are brothers, and blood
Relationships so often turn sour. I hate
All that, that sibling rivalry   510
And family feuding, I reject it as unworthy.
But. The fact is. Your generosity doesn't help.
We are boxed in by circumstances, or like an animal in a
                                                        net.
There is no alternative. I must murder my child.

MENELAUS.

No! Why? Your own child? What compels you to do it?

AGAMEMNON.

This whole Greek army, in camp all round us.

MENELAUS.

No, it doesn't. Not if you send her back home.

AGAMEMNON.

She might escape in secret. I can't.

MENELAUS.

Ignore the rabble! They don't matter.

AGAMEMNON.

Calchas will go public. The whole army will know.

MENELAUS.

Not if we kill him first. It's possible.

AGAMEMNON.

520 God damn all ambitious political priests!

MENELAUS.

They're useless to man or beast . . . while they live.

AGAMEMNON.

The possibilities are terrifying. Don't they frighten you?

MENELAUS.

I don't know, till you tell me what they are.

AGAMEMNON.

Odysseus, of Sisyphus' clan, he knows everything.

MENELAUS.

So what? Odysseus can't hurt us two.

AGAMEMNON.

He's crafty. And very popular with the troops.

MENELAUS.

He's consumed with ambition. That can be dangerous.

AGAMEMNON.

Don't you think he'll make the most
Of his opportunity? He'll stand up in front
Of the whole army, and explain every detail

Of Calchas' prophecy, line by line!
He'll tell them I promised to go along with it
And make the sacrifice, and then retracted   530
My promise. With that sort of speech
In our situation, he could stage a coup,
Take command of the army, and have us both killed,
As well as the girl. And if we escaped,
What could stop him bringing the whole army
To Argos, Cyclops-built walls and all,
Taking the place by storm, killing me and mine
And occupying the whole country?
With an army this size, it's possible, I have
To take it into account. So you see
What an appalling situation I'm in,
How utterly I'm trapped. I despair
Of any solution, save a stoical acceptance
Of the will of the gods, whatever that costs me.
But one thing, Menelaus, you can do for me.
Speak to everybody important in the army,
Make sure that Clytemnestra doesn't hear
A single word about this – or not before   540
I've taken the child away from her
And seen the whole business through . . . when she's dead
I mean. That way at least, I'll be able
To do this evil thing I have to do
With the minimum of tears. And you, foreign women
From Chalcis, keep silent! If you value your lives.

Exeunt AGAMEMNON *and* MENELAUS.

CHORUS.

Those people are happy who relish love's pleasure,
Enjoying Aphrodite's sensual embrace
As a ship riding easy on a calm sea,
Avoiding the obsession that leads to disgrace.
For sex, like a horsefly, can madden with its sting,
And Eros has two arrows to his string,
Beneath that deceptive golden hair.
A mere scratch from the first brings lifelong joy,   550
But the second wounds to death, and breeds despair.

Goddess born in Cyprus, keep my bedroom safe
From that mortal arrow, make love in my life
A steady continuing delight,
Not obsessional or destructive. Let me serve
The great Queen with ecstasy, as is her right,
But commit no crimes for her, nor become her slave.

The deepest secret of human nature
Is variety. There are as many ways
Of living as there are men and women to live them;
But the morality of the good life obeys
The simplest of principles: it is clear,
560   Straightforward and comprehensible. The wise never fear
Life's disasters, if virtue has been their discipline
From childhood. To judge from a moral standpoint,
Even in details, brings stability to strangers and kin,
And there is no satisfaction like doing what is to be done
Properly and well. Reputation is won,
Even fame, that way, and such fame endures.
For women, a loving and chaste fidelity
570   Is Aphrodite's most secret joy. A man secures,
Through all the variety of his gifts, fame through integrity.

Paris, you returned to the place of your birth
As a shepherd upon Mount Ida's slopes
Where the white heifers graze.
You played the folk melodies of your native earth
On the Phrygian flute, whose simple stops
Olympus invented in legendary days.

Full of milk the cattle grazed
580   When the goddesses chose you: and that choice
Drove you like a man possessed to Greece,
To a palace of inlaid ivory, where you stood amazed
At the beauty of Helen's eyes,
Fed deep upon them, and saw desire
Burn there, like the uncontrollable fire
Consuming your own heart: ecstasies
That caused these men to march and ships deploy,

For two goddesses' injured pride, to shatter with chariot
and spear
The citadels and towers of Troy.

Enter CLYTEMNESTRA *and* IPHIGENIA *with attendants,
and a* NURSE, *who carries the baby* ORESTES. *Also a
second* CHORUS *of soldiers.*

SOLDIERS.

Look now, they're coming, the fortunate   590
Ones, the aristocrats, the masters of the earth,
Princess Iphigenia, the King's daughter, and the great
Queen Clytemnestra, whose illustrious birth
Blessed Tyndareus' family. Their happy fate
Sets them at the summit of good fortune and wealth.
Power is theirs, and glory, like gods to create
Pleasure or pain, plenty or dearth.

CHORUS.

Women of Chalcis, stand
Close by the chariot, offer
To the Queen a helping hand.
She must not stumble. Give her
Gentle support with your arm
Till she's safe on the ground. And Iphigenia,   600
Agamemnon's famous daughter, have no fear.
We are strangers too. There's no cause for alarm.
Strangers from Argos will be welcome here.

CLYTEMNESTRA.

This warm greeting and courteous speech
Of welcome, promises good luck,
As much as any fortunate pattern
Of birds in flight. And I have certainly
Come here with the best of expectations, to bring
This bride to a most suitable and happy marriage!   610
I have brought wedding-gifts as a dowry.
Unload them from the cart with the greatest care
And take them into this building!
And now, my dear girl, so like a child still,
So tender and fragile: step down carefully,
And you women, take her hand, help her from the carriage

Safely . . . don't fall! And then, one of you
Hold out an arm to support me, so that I
Can get down from my seat with reasonable grace.
For heaven's sake, some of you stand
By the horses' heads, and take their attention!
620   You know how they panic if something takes their eye
In strange surroundings! Talk to them,
Calm them down!
                                    And now, the child,
The son of Agamemnon, hold out your arms
For him! His name is Orestes. He's not talking
Yet, a tiny baby still, you see?
There. My dear little boy, you're asleep
Aren't you, the rocking of the carriage
Made you nod off . . . Wake up, little fellow,
To wish your sister good luck. The son
Of a fine man, himself a tremendous fellow,
Whose mother was a sea nymph, one of the Nereids,
Is going to marry her.
                                    Come here, my child,
Take your place close by your mother,
Sit there, Iphigenia, as a daughter should,
To show these people what a lucky woman I am
In my children, and what a family group
We make together.

Enter AGAMEMNON.

                                    But look, here's your father.
630   Stand up child, show how pleased you are to see him.

IPHIGENIA.
Don't be angry with me if I beat you to it
Mother, and cuddle him tight before you do . . .

CLYTEMNESTRA.
Not yet child!
                    My Lord and Master, godlike
Agamemnon, we are here, as you commanded us to be.

IPHIGENIA.
But I must be first, Father, to hold you

In my arms after so long, just to look at you.
I've missed you so much! Mother, don't be angry!

CLYTEMNESTRA.
No. This is just as it should be. Of all
My children, you've always loved your father most.

IPHIGENIA.
I'm so happy, Father, it's been such a long time . . .   640

AGAMEMNON.
And for me, I feel just the same as you do . . .

IPHIGENIA.
You did the right thing, Daddy, bringing me here.

AGAMEMNON.
Perhaps so . . . I don't know what to say. Perhaps not.

IPHIGENIA.
What . . . ?
Why look at me like that, if you're so glad to see me?

AGAMEMNON.
A King . . . a General . . . has many things on his mind.

IPHIGENIA.
Forget all that now. This moment is all mine!

AGAMEMNON.
All yours then, for one moment . . . No responsibilities.

IPHIGENIA.
Smooth away those frowns then, fill your eyes with love!

AGAMEMNON.
I am as happy to see you child, as I can possibly be.

IPHIGENIA.
Don't cry then! There's no need to cry now.   650

AGAMEMNON.
We'll be parted too soon. For a long time.

IPHIGENIA.
How can you say so! What do you mean?

AGAMEMNON.
You speak . . . so honestly. I can't hold back my tears.

IPHIGENIA.

I'll talk nonsense then, if that makes you feel better!

AGAMEMNON.

Dear God, how can I not tell her . . . ? Thank you my
                                            dear.

IPHIGENIA.

Don't go Father. Stay at home with your children.

AGAMEMNON.

I would love to. But I can't. And it's agony for me.

IPHIGENIA.

To hell with all wars, and Menelaus and his troubles!

AGAMEMNON.

Many men will go to Hell for him. Me too, in the end.

IPHIGENIA.

660   You've been here in the Bay of Aulis too long . . .

AGAMEMNON.

We should sail at once. But . . . something prevents us.

IPHIGENIA.

Where do they say they live, Father, these Trojans?

AGAMEMNON.

Where Paris lives, Priam's son. I wish to God he didn't . . .

IPHIGENIA.

It's a long journey then; and you're leaving me behind!

AGAMEMNON.

Yours is a long journey too, like mine.

IPHIGENIA.

We could travel together then. You could arrange it.

AGAMEMNON.

No, your journey is different. You must remember me.

IPHIGENIA.

Will my mother sail with me? Or must I travel alone?

AGAMEMNON.

You'll sail alone . . . without father or mother.

IPHIGENIA.

670   Have you found me a new home, Father? Where is it?

AGAMEMNON.
>That's enough . . . There are some things young girls
>>shouldn't know.

IPHIGENIA.
>Sort the Phrygians out quickly, Daddy, and come back
>>to me.

AGAMEMNON.
>I must perform a sacrifice, before I go.

IPHIGENIA.
>Of course you must! The right sacred rituals.

AGAMEMNON.
>You'll be there too. By the holy water.

IPHIGENIA.
>Shall I be part of the ceremonies at the altar?

AGAMEMNON.
>What wouldn't I give to be as blessedly innocent
>As you are . . . ? Go inside now, child.
>You shouldn't be seen in public, only by your women.
>But . . . give me a kiss first, hold my hand tight!
>You'll soon be gone away from me, a long way,
>And for too long a time . . . Your bosom is so soft,   680
>Your cheeks so fresh and childlike, your golden hair . . .
>That city of the Phrygians, and Helen,
>Why should they lay such a savage weight
>Of responsibility on you . . . ! I must stop,
>Stop talking like this . . . Even to touch you
>Suddenly makes me cry, in spite of myself . . .
>Go into my headquarters . . . .

Exit IPHIGENIA.

>>>>>My apologies to you,
>Daughter of Leda, the thought of losing
>My daughter . . . to Achilles . . . breaks my heart.
>Partings of this kind are happy ones, of course,
>But for the parents, and the father particularly,
>To give his daughter to another man
>After bringing her up with so much love
690 >And care for so long, can't help being painful.

CLYTEMNESTRA.
    Of course, I understand. You may be sure
    I shall feel equally heartbroken
    When I hear the wedding hymns sung for my daughter;
    So I can hardly blame you for feeling now
    What I shall feel then. But time and custom
    Will ease the pain. I know the name
    Of the man you have engaged to be married
    To my child. But is he of good family?
    Where is he from? I should like to know.

AGAMEMNON.
    Aesopus had a daughter, named Aegina.

CLYTEMNESTRA.
    And who married her? A man, or a god?

AGAMEMNON.
    It was Zeus. He fathered Aeacus, the ruler of Oenone.

CLYTEMNESTRA.
700   And which of his sons inherited the property?

AGAMEMNON.
    Peleus, who married a sea nymph, Nereus' daughter.

CLYTEMNESTRA.
    With the gods' agreement, or in spite of them?

AGAMEMNON.
    Zeus himself made the match. He gave her away.

CLYTEMNESTRA.
    And where did he marry this sea nymph? Underwater?

AGAMEMNON.
    On the sacred slopes of Mount Pelion: Chiron's home.

CLYTEMNESTRA.
    Where the Centaurs live, half man half horse – so they say.

AGAMEMNON.
    The gods held a banquet there, in Peleus' honour.

CLYTEMNESTRA.
    And who brought up Achilles? Thetis, or his father?

AGAMEMNON.
Chiron taught him . . . to avoid the wickedness of men.

CLYTEMNESTRA.
Oh wise teacher . . . and even wiser father.   710

AGAMEMNON.
This is the man who will marry your daughter.

CLYTEMNESTRA.
He could hardly be bettered. Is his home town in Greece?

AGAMEMNON.
In the mountains of Phthia, on the river Apidanos.

CLYTEMNESTRA.
And that's where you'll take your daughter – and mine –

AGAMEMNON.
That'll be his business, when he's married to her.

CLYTEMNESTRA.
My best wishes to them both. When's the wedding day?

AGAMEMNON.
The next full moon. For good luck.

CLYTEMNESTRA.
Have you made the blood sacrifice to Artemis, for her sake?

AGAMEMNON.
I am about to. The matter is well in hand.

CLYTEMNESTRA.
The wedding feast itself, will that be held later?   720

AGAMEMNON.
Yes. The sacrifice to the gods must come first.

CLYTEMNESTRA.
And where shall I hold the womenfolk's party?

AGAMEMNON.
Here. In the shadow of the Greek ships.

CLYTEMNESTRA.
A case of take it or leave it. Well, we must hope for the
                                                    best.

AGAMEMNON.
You know what is required of you. Please do as I say!

CLYTEMNESTRA.
Yes, perfectly! I ought to, by now.

AGAMEMNON.
Meanwhile, we . . . the men . . . in the bridegroom's
presence —

CLYTEMNESTRA.
Will do what? Without me? It's a mother's business.

AGAMEMNON.
Before the Greek army . . . I shall give away my daughter.

730   CLYTEMNESTRA.
And where, pray, shall I be, while all this is going on?

AGAMEMNON.
Back in Argos. Looking after your other girls.

CLYTEMNESTRA.
Leaving my daughter? I must light her wedding torches . . .

AGAMEMNON.
I shall light the flames myself . . . for the marriage, I
mean . . .

CLYTEMNESTRA.
That's unheard of, an outrage to all decency!

AGAMEMNON.
It's an outrage to see women in an army encampment.

CLYTEMNESTRA.
It's a mother's duty to see her children married!

AGAMEMNON.
It's her duty to look after her daughters at home.

CLYTEMNESTRA.
They're quite safe, well guarded, in the women's wing.

AGAMEMNON.
Listen . . .

CLYTEMNESTRA.
No, by the greatest goddess of the Greeks!

You give your orders out here. Domestic affairs, 740
Including my daughter's marriage, are my business!

Exit CLYTEMNESTRA *and her entourage.*

AGAMEMNON.
Well. God help me, that little plan
Blew up in my face! To get my wife
Out of the way was the first necessity,
And I failed to do even that! Even a conspiracy
Against my nearest and dearest proves
More than I can handle. I must talk to Calchas,
Find out exactly what the goddess demands,
And if this personal disaster, and shameful calamity
For the whole Greek nation, is in any way
Avoidable . . . A sensible man
Keeps a quiet, reliable, domestic wife
Who stays at home – or no wife at all. 750

Exit AGAMEMNON.

CHORUS.
Now, to the silvery waters and swirling
Currents of the river Simois, the Greeks
Will come, with their massive fleet,
Landing cavalry divisions and uncounted ranks
Of heavy infantry, assembling
A terrible war machine on the plains of Troy,
The city sacred to Apollo.
And already I can hear the god-driven shout
Of Cassandra, as she lashes her yellow
Laurel-crowned hair like a whip, and the voice of
                                          prophecy 760
Weeps at the horrors it sees in its visionary frenzy.

On the battle towers of Troy, and along the walls
Encircling the city, the whole nation
Of Trojans will stand watching,
Awestruck, as if the war god himself led the invasion
Of bronze shields like mirrored fire from the sea, the
                                          rhythmic falls
Of rank upon rank of disciplined oars, powering

The high prowed troopships to the many-channelled mouth
Of Simois, one burning desire driving
All this machinery of war: that Helen, by birth
770   Sister of the Heavenly Twins, should be dragged, protesting
Or not, by force of Greek swords and shields, to a grim
                                                    homecoming.

Then the vengeful Greek army will draw
A circle of blood round the stone towers
Of Pergamon, the rich Phrygian city
The world knows as Troy. Both the wretch who cowers
In the shadows, and Paris himself, will be hauled out by the
                                                    hair

And their naked throats severed, or slashed to the ear,
As the columns totter, and the rafters crash
And the whole great city is flattened. The screaming
Of womenfolk, young girls' sobbing, gasps for pity
Even from Priam's Queen, will be drowned in a flood of
780   weeping,

And Helen herself, Zeus' daughter, in the ash
Of her burned out dreams, will understand that rash
Actions have fearful consequences, and the fatal dowry
To be paid for leaving a husband. My most passionate
                                                    prayer
Is that neither my children nor grandchildren should ever
                                                    wash
Their eyes with such tears as the gold robed Lydians will
                                          weep, or know the fear
Of the millionaire wives of Troy, as they stand by their
                                                    looms and cry,

790   'Who is the man who will drag me by the hair
Till the tears start from my eyes
And tear me by the roots from my native earth
As a hooligan tears up a flower, while my homeland dies
All round me? The author of our despair
Is you, daughter of the long-necked swan.
For Zeus, the story says, assumed the shape
Of a white-winged bird to bring your beauty to birth,
If the legend's true of the immortal rape

Of Leda. Unless poets weave their fantasies in vain,
Hoping with childish dreams to soothe our pain.'   800

Enter ACHILLES.

ACHILLES.
Where is the Supreme Commander of the Greek
Expeditionary Force? Is this his headquarters?
You there, aide, staff officer,
Or whatever you are, tell him Achilles,
The son of Peleus is here, and must see him.
This hanging about by the Straits of Euripus
Inconveniences some men more than others.
Some of us are not yet married, have left
Our fathers at home, undefended, and sit here
Idly sunbathing on the beach. While married men
Have wives and families to consider. It's strange,
This obsession to join the expedition
Against Troy, how it possesses everyone.
It's the gods' business we do here, for sure,
They guide our hands. But I speak for myself –   810
Any other man can say what he likes –
And my complaint is that I've left Pharsalus
And my old guv'nor Peleus, and now I'm stuck
Here, waiting for the merest breeze
To ripple the Straits of Euripus, with my crack
Regiment, the Myrmidons, sitting on their hands!
Day after day they grouse at me.
'Achilles,' they say, 'what are we waiting for,
How much longer must we wait for our little trip to Troy?
Do something, if you can, or else
Let's all go home, instead of wasting time
Here, while the two sons of Atreus try
To make up their minds, and, as usual, fail!'

Enter CLYTEMNESTRA.

CLYTEMNESTRA.
Even from inside, Son of the sea goddess,
I heard what you were saying, and I came out at once.   820

ACHILLES.
Spare my blushes, goddess of good manners,
At the approach of such a handsome woman!

CLYTEMNESTRA.
You don't know me . . . that's not surprising,
We've never met. But thank you for your courtesy.

ACHILLES.
Who are you? And what are you doing here,
In the Greek camp, surrounded by armed men?

CLYTEMNESTRA.
I am Leda's daughter. Clytemnestra is my name.
The King Agamemnon is my husband.

ACHILLES.
Well, that's brief and to the point, just as it should be.
830 Can't talk here with a woman. Much too embarrassing.

CLYTEMNESTRA.
Wait . . . don't run away! Take my right hand
In yours, and pray for a happy marriage!

ACHILLES.
I beg your pardon? You want me to hold hands
With Agamemnon's wife? That's really not done!

CLYTEMNESTRA.
Of course it is, it's perfectly right and proper
Since you're marrying my daughter! Son of the sea nymph!

ACHILLES.
I'm marrying . . . I'm speechless . . . What are you talking
about?
Are you making it up? Or are you mad?

CLYTEMNESTRA.
Naturally, you're embarrassed. Everyone is
When marriage is on the cards, and they meet their new
840 relations.

ACHILLES.
Madam, I'm not marrying anybody! I've never
Even met your daughter, and the Atreus brothers have said
nothing.

CLYTEMNESTRA.
  What does this mean? I can see that my words
  Come as a surprise to you. Yours leave me staggered.
ACHILLES.
  Just a moment now . . . Let's think. Put both heads
  together.
  Maybe neither of us is talking nonsense?
CLYTEMNESTRA.
  It seems I have been made a fool of. Travelling
  To celebrate a non-existent marriage. How insulting!
ACHILLES.
  Someone has made a fool of both of us. So . . .
  That's a mere bagatelle. Don't take it to heart.   850
CLYTEMNESTRA.
  No sir, goodbye. I've been humiliated,
  And made to seem a liar. I can't look you in the face . . .
ACHILLES.
  Goodbye to you too Madam. I'm going inside
  That headquarters building, to find your husband!
  Enter the OLD MAN.
OLD MAN.
  Sir . . . just a minute . . . Aeacus' grandson, aren't you,
  Son of a goddess . . . And you too, Daughter of Leda!
ACHILLES.
  Who's that in the doorway, too scared to speak out loud?
OLD MAN.
  A slave, Sir, with no pretensions. I know my place.
ACHILLES.
  Whose slave? None of my people work for Agamemnon.
OLD MAN.
  Her's Sir, over there. I came with her, from
  Tyndareus.   860
ACHILLES.
  Well, I'm waiting. If you've anything to say, say it.
OLD MAN.
  Are you two alone out there, in front of the doors?

ACHILLES.
Yes we are. You can speak. Come away from the hut.

OLD MAN.
With good luck, and good thinking, I shall save someone's
life!

ACHILLES.
This old man knows something. Something important.

CLYTEMNESTRA.
If you've something to tell me . . . don't bother with hand
kissing.

OLD MAN.
You know me, my Lady, loyal to you and your daughter.

CLYTEMNESTRA.
Yes, one of the house serfs in my father's palace.

OLD MAN.
And I came to Lord Agamemnon as part of your dowry.

CLYTEMNESTRA.
Yes, you travelled to Argos with me, you've always been
870   mine.

OLD MAN.
And my loyalty's to you, Ma'am, more than your husband.

CLYTEMNESTRA.
Speak out then. If you've some secret information . . .

OLD MAN.
Your daughter . . . her own father . . . The murderer . . .
he plans to kill her!

CLYTEMNESTRA.
What! I'll choke you with those words, old man! Are you
mad?

OLD MAN.
With a knife he'll do it. Cut her poor white throat!

CLYTEMNESTRA.
God help me! My husband! Is the man insane?

OLD MAN.
He's sane enough, except about you and your daughter.

CLYTEMNESTRA.
For what reason? What possesses him to do such a thing?

OLD MAN.
The gods demand it, Calchas says, before the fleet can sail.

CLYTEMNESTRA.
Sail where? I'm his wife! How can he? She's his
daughter! 880

OLD MAN.
To Troy, so that Menelaus can drag Helen back home.

CLYTEMNESTRA.
So must my Iphigenia die to ransom Helen?

OLD MAN.
That's the gist. Her father will sacrifice your child to
Artemis.

CLYTEMNESTRA.
So the marriage was a pretext, to persuade me to bring her
here.

OLD MAN.
So you'd be happy to bring her, to marry her to Achilles.

CLYTEMNESTRA.
My daughter! I've brought you to your destruction. And
mine!

OLD MAN.
It's terrible for both of you. But that Agamemnon should
dare . . .

CLYTEMNESTRA.
This is agony . . . I can't stay here . . . I'm going to
cry . . .

OLD MAN.
Who can hold back their tears, when a child dies?

CLYTEMNESTRA.
Old man . . . where . . . ? I mean . . . listen . . . how did
you find out . . . ? 890

OLD MAN.
I was on the way to you, with a second letter.

CLYTEMNESTRA.
Confirming or cancelling the order to bring her to her
death?

OLD MAN.
Telling you not to bring her. He was thinking straight then.

CLYTEMNESTRA.
Then why . . . with such a message, didn't you deliver it?

OLD MAN.
Menelaus intercepted it. He caused this disaster!

CLYTEMNESTRA.
Do you hear, Thetis' child, son of Peleus, these infamies?

ACHILLES.
For you, unendurable. And for me, an insult!

CLYTEMNESTRA.
They use marriage to Achilles to lure my daughter to her
death!

ACHILLES.
Your husband has angered me. That is not a small
matter . . .

CLYTEMNESTRA.
900   I'm not ashamed to fall on my knees
Before you, son of a sea goddess as you are.
I am a mortal woman, and this is not time
To stand on ceremony or the protocol of rank.
I'll do anything, humiliate myself at your feet
If necessary, for my daughter's sake.
Stand up for me, son of Thetis,
Defend me from this unmerited disaster,
And stand up for your wife, wife in name only
Admittedly, but none the less yours for all that.
I brought her here with flowers in her hair,
As I thought, to a marriage: and in truth I've led her
Like a sacrificial victim to the slaughter.
Some of the blame will fall on you
For certain, if you do nothing to save her.
You may not be married, but it was common knowledge

That you were to be the poor girl's husband.
By everything that makes you a man, your strong right arm,
Your manly beard, your mother's good name,
Your own good reputation – because it was the glory   910
Of your name that brought us to this danger –
Save your own honour by saving us.
No god can help me, I can only abase myself
Here, at your knees, as though they were an altar,
And clasp them with my prayers. I have no friends,
And the unscrupulous savagery of Agamemnon's plan
You know now as well as I do. I have come here,
A woman, in a military base
Full of soldiers and marines, whose lawlessness
Is a byword, and whose casual violence
Makes every kind of evil-doing commonplace.
And yet that anarchic energy too can be harnessed
In a good cause, if ... can convince them.
If you have the courage to lift up your right arm
In our defence, we'll be saved, for sure!
If not, that's our last hope of salvation gone.

CHORUS.

Giving birth is the deepest of life's mysteries:
No animal fights fiercer than a mother for her child.

ACHILLES.

All my most noble qualities are inflamed
To immediate action: but I am mature enough   920
To understand the virtues of moderation, both
In the anguish of grief and the exhilaration of triumph.
Such men as I am are universally acknowledged
To act coolly, with good judgement, and according to
                                             reason.
There are certain times when one should act by instinct,
Without too much thought. But there are also times
When one must think sensibly, and exercise one's
                                             intelligence.
I was schooled by Chiron, a godfearing man
Who brought me up to be straightforward,
A direct, decent, uncomplicated fellow.

If the sons of Atreus command the army sensibly,
I shall obey them. If they don't, I won't.
930   Both here and at Troy, I shall be my own man,
And bring some honour to the god of war
With my sword too, you may be sure.
As for you, my dear madam, who have suffered so cruelly
At the hands of your nearest and dearest, everything
A young man can do, I shall do
To remove the cause of your suffering.
My generosity of spirit will protect you like a shield,
And your daughter will certainly not be killed by her father
Now she is engaged to me! I shall never allow him
To use me as a mere instrument
In the manufacturing of his conspiracies!
If I did, my name would have murdered your daughter
As surely as any sword. But the guilt
940   Is your husband's, not mine. The very blood
In my veins would be infected, polluted
With murder, if this girl should suffer
Such an intolerable injustice,
And on my account, because of marriage to me,
Be herself destroyed. What would I be worth then?
Nothing at all, the most despicable worm
In the whole Greek camp. Even Menelaus
Would seem a man beside me!
If my name were to become your husband's mercenary
And do his killing for him, some demon
Of destruction must have been my ancestor,
Not Peleus! No, by that son of the Ocean,
Nereus, the father of my mother Thetis,
950   King Agamemnon, I swear, will not lay a finger
Even on the hem of your daughter's dress,
Much less touch her! Otherwise, call the wilderness
Of Mount Sipylus, where the barbarians live,
And where his family came from, a great city,
And may my own home of Phthia be forever forgotten
In the mouths of men! Calchas, no doubt,
Will bring all his little jugs and basins
To mystify us. But what does a priest matter?

At best he speaks a few fragments of truth
In a whole rubbish dump of lies.
And when his prophecies prove total nonsense
He keeps himself well out of sight!
It's not for the marriage I'm making all this fuss.
Thousands of girls are desperate for the chance   960
To get into bed with me. It's because
King Agamemnon has insulted me!
If he wanted to use my name as a snare
To trap his own child, he should have asked my permission!
It was my reputation that attracted Clytemnestra
To bring her daughter here, not her husband's command.
If the Greeks had asked for the use of my name
To make the trip to Troy possible,
I wouldn't have refused them, not my fellow soldiers,
My colleagues in this great venture. But as it is
These generals treat me as a nonentity,
As though whether they honour or shame me
Were a matter of not the slightest concern
To either of them! But anyone who tries
To take your daughter away from me
Will be practice meat for my iron sword,
To see how bloodstains suit the blade   970
Before I go to Troy! Don't be frightened.
I know I must seem like a god, and a very great one
At that! In fact, I'm a man, not a god,
Though by my actions I shall certainly become one!

CHORUS.
That speech was worthy of you, son of Peleus!
And of your mother, whose cradle was the sea!

CLYTEMNESTRA.
How can I find the right words
To express my gratitude, or to eulogise you
As you deserve, without embarrassing you
With flattery, or offending you
By undervaluing your virtues?
The best men hate those who overpraise them,   980
And I feel ashamed to be burdening you

With my private anguish. The pain is all mine,
It's my heart that's breaking, not yours.
And yet, there is something admirable
When a good man stoops from his own good fortune
To help someone less fortunate.
Take pity on me, because my case is pitiable!
I thought you were going to be my son-in-law.
A pathetic illusion that turned out to be!
But think what bad luck it would be for you
In your future marriage to remember
The circumstances of my daughter's death
And your part in it! You should do everything
990   Possible to avoid that. What you said first
Was to the point, and what you said last.
If you choose to save her, my child will be saved.
Shall I bring her out here, shall she kneel
At your feet and beg for her life? It's not right
To make an unmarried girl do such a thing,
But she'll do it, if that's what you want.
With her eyes decently lowered too,
Not brazenly, staring, like a whore,
But with a modest nobility, as becomes a princess.
If I can persuade you, without seeing her,
Let her preserve her modesty indoors.
But if she must come out, she'll come.

ACHILLES.
No, don't bring her out just for me to get a look at her!
Nor, dear lady, should we give stupid people
The opportunity to laugh at us.
1000   The soldiers have nothing to do, the whole army
Is unemployed, and unrestrained too
By being away from home. They love nothing better
Than malicious gossip. It's irrelevant to me
Whether you implore me on your knees or not.
I've made up my mind that I shall save you
At whatever cost, from this disaster!
Listen to me, take good note of what I say.
I never lie. If I prove a liar,

Or my promises worthless, let me die on the spot.
You have my word that I will save your child!

CLYTEMNESTRA.
The heavens bless you for helping people in trouble.

ACHILLES.
Now listen, this is what I want you to do.

CLYTEMNESTRA.
What do you suggest? I have no choice but to listen.   1010

ACHILLES.
We'll persuade her father to have second thoughts.

CLYTEMNESTRA.
But that's hopeless! He's a coward. He's scared of the army!

ACHILLES.
But good arguments, like good wrestlers, overcome the bad!

CLYTEMNESTRA.
There's cold comfort in that. But tell me what I must do.

ACHILLES.
First, go down on your knees and beg him
Not to kill your child. If he won't listen
Come straight back to me. If he does listen,
And agrees with what you say, I need not do anything,
Since by that very action the problem will be solved.
In that case too, my relations with your husband
Wouldn't be compromised, would indeed become closer,
And the army at large could hardly criticise me   1020
If I achieved all this by diplomacy, not force.
That would be a satisfactory outcome
For all of us, for you, and for our friends,
And I need not be involved at all.

CLYTEMNESTRA.
You give sensible advice, I'm sure,
Counselling restraint, and I shall act upon it.
But supposing he ignores me, or gives me nothing
In return for my pleading, what then?
Where shall I see you? My situation

Will be desperate. You're the only man
Who can possibly help me. Where shall I find you?

ACHILLES.

When you need me I shall be there,
Never fear! But make sure no one sees you
1030   Making a fuss through the whole Greek camp
Looking for me. That would be a disgrace . . .
To your father Tyndareus, who's a good fellow
With a very high reputation among the Greeks.
Don't let him down, or slander his good name.

CLYTEMNESTRA.

Of course, you're right. You take command,
I'll do what you say. If the gods
Exist at all, they must surely reward
Such a principled stand as yours. And if not . . .
Then everything is meaningless, and nothing worth doing.

Exeunt CLYTEMNESTRA *and* ACHILLES.

CHORUS.

What a joyful wedding song they sang,
How wildly the music of instruments rang,
The sighing African flute
And the soft voice of the lute,
While the dancers' beating feet
Kept time with the song,
And the oboes sang shrill and sweet;
When to Peleus' wedding feast
The nine muses came
On Pelion's high pasture, a host
1040   Whose fair hair swung to the beat
Of their golden sandalled feet,
Singing in praise of Thetis' name
A song so melodious it carried her fame
And her husband, Aeacus' son, beyond Pelion's hills
Where the Centaurs gallop, and the green forest sleeps.
Phrygian Prince Ganymede heard it, and fills
Zeus' cup from the wine bowl's golden deeps,
Dardanus' son, Zeus' favourite, and never spills

The nectar: and in honour of marriage, circling hand
                                        in hand,   1050
The fifty daughters of Nereus danced on the white sea-sand.

Half horses, half men, to where the gods lay feasting,
Their heads crowned with leaves, the Centaurs came riding,
Each with a lance of pine,
To drink the immortal wine
In Bacchus' golden bowl   1060
At the sea nymph's wedding.
With one voice they call,
'Good luck to Nereus' daughter!
Chiron, who can see
The mind of Apollo, has brought her
News of a son she will bear
Whose name will be known everywhere,
A great light, shining from Thessaly.
He will lead his Myrmidons over the sea
To Troy, to blast with spear and shield and fire
Priam's great city, in helmet and breastplate of gold,   1070
Hephaestos' masterpiece, such as the gods wear,
His mother's parting gift to her bold
Son.' Was such feasting seen ever before?
The gods sat at table, in immortal company,
When Peleus married the Nereid, first-born child of the sea.

But you, Iphigenia,   1080
On your flowing hair, on your golden hair,
Greek soldiers will set a crown of flowers
As they garland a heifer for the knife and fire,
Pure from the mountain, dappled red and white.
Warm blood from the trembling throat
They will draw, and that blood will be yours,
Not from a beast bred where the herdsman whistles and
                                        sings,
But a girl her mother nurtured to be bride and mother of
                                        Kings.

Crimson the face of shame.   1090
Can goodness prevail, can virtue prevail?
A godless generation is in power.

Where is decency, who speaks her name?
Lost in the crowd, trampled to death,
Stifled, choked by the stinking breath
Of self interest, in this darkest hour
When the fear of God is dead, brotherhood gone rotten,
And the vengeance the jealous gods exact from men

                                                    forgotten.

Enter CLYTEMNESTRA.

CLYTEMNESTRA.
I've come out here to look for my husband.
He left the headquarters some time ago,
And hasn't been seen since. My poor child
1100   Is in tears, if you can call it that,
Such moaning and screams of despair and anguish.
She knows the truth now: that her father plans to kill her.
But . . . talk of the devil . . . here he comes,
Agamemnon, that father who will now be exposed
As guilty of planning the most unnatural crime
Of all, the murder of his own child.

Enter AGAMEMNON.

AGAMEMNON.
Ah, daughter of Leda, I'm glad to catch you here
Outside the building. I have things to tell you
While Iphigenia is inside, things not suitable
For a young girl to hear just before her wedding . . .

CLYTEMNESTRA.
What things, only suitable to be said outside?

AGAMEMNON.
1110   Send the girl out here. Tell her her father
Is waiting . . . and everything is prepared.
The chalices are ready, and the barley meal
We sprinkle to purify the altar fire.
The victim is ready too. Her red blood
Must spurt from a pure white neck in honour
Of Artemis, to celebrate the marriage.

CLYTEMNESTRA.
Yes, fine words, it all sounds most admirable;
But what words will describe your admirable actions,
How fine will they be? My daughter! Come out here!
You know it all now. All your father's plans.
And your baby brother Orestes, bring him too,
Wrap him snugly in the folds of your dress . . .

IPHIGENIA *enters, carrying the baby* ORESTES.

CLYTEMNESTRA.
So. Here she is. Obeying you to the letter.   1120
Now I shall speak. For her, and for myself.

AGAMEMNON.
My child. Why are you crying? No more
Smiles for me now? All downcast looks,
Wiping your eyes with the hem of your gown?

CLYTEMNESTRA.
Dear gods . . .
How shall I begin? With pain like this
There's no beginning, middle or ending.
Wherever you start, it's the same agony!

AGAMEMNON.
What's this all about? You must have rehearsed
This tearful performance together, I think.

CLYTEMNESTRA.
One question, husband. Answer it like a man.

AGAMEMNON.
Don't give me orders . . . ! Of course I'll answer . . .

CLYTEMNESTRA.
Your daughter. My daughter. Are you going to kill her?

AGAMEMNON.
Am I *what*?
What an appalling question, how foul of you to suspect . . .

CLYTEMNESTRA.
Be quiet,
Just answer it. I can't put it more simply.

AGAMEMNON.
Ask a reasonable question, you'll get a rational answer . . .

CLYTEMNESTRA.
1130   That question, no other! And I want a straight answer.

AGAMEMNON.
My destiny, my bad luck! I've done nothing to deserve this!

CLYTEMNESTRA.
My bad luck, and hers! All three of us, the same!

AGAMEMNON.
Have I wronged you?

CLYTEMNESTRA.
You ask me that?
Have you any brains left, or are you quite stupid?

AGAMEMNON.
1140   I'm finished . . . no chance . . . they know everything . . .

CLYTEMNESTRA.
Yes, I know it all, the whole filthy plan.
And this silence of yours, this muttering in your beard
Is as good as a confession. You don't need to say anything!

AGAMEMNON.
Am I trying to speak? There's nothing more to say.
Why add to the disaster by telling lies about it?

CLYTEMNESTRA.
Then you listen to me, it's my turn now
And there'll be no obscurity or riddling
In what I have to say, just plain words,
That you don't dare deny! In the first place –
And what a shameful beginning that was –
You married me against my will,
1150   Took me by force, killed my first husband,
Tantalus, dragged my baby from my breast . . .
And smashed its head open on the ground . . .
My brothers, the twin sons of Zeus,
Shining like a vision on their white horses,
Led an army against you. And you grovelled

Before my old father, Tyndareus, his diplomacy
Saved your life, and even got you back into my bed
As my second husband. And from that very day
When I reconciled myself to marriage with you
You can appear as my principal witness
When I say that I have been a model wife,
Both personally to you, and in organising your house,
Sexually modest, and utterly chaste,
So that coming home has always been your greatest
                                  pleasure   1160
And when you open your front door, the whole world can
                                  see
Your good fortune demonstrated. Bad wives are
                                  commonplace,
Never in short supply. But it's a lucky man
That has such a wife as I have been to you.
I have borne you three girls, and finally, this son;
And now, without feeling or conscience
You will tear one of my girls from me,
Like ripping the flesh from my own body.
And if anyone asks you why you will kill her,
For what good reason, what will you say?
Shall I say it for you? So that Menelaus
Can have Helen back! What a glorious action,
To ransom a whore with a child's life,
To buy back, with what is most precious,
The commonest, cheapest thing in the world!   1170
So. You do that, and go off to war,
For years perhaps, leaving me here
At home. How do you think I will feel
Alone in the house, whenever I see
Her empty chair, her empty bedroom
In the children's wing? Shall I sit on my own
With red eyes, always singing the same sad song,
'Your father killed you, little girl,
He gave you your life, and then he took it,
No hired killer, but his own hand
Put an end to your life; what welcome,
What homecoming for him, my little girl?'

1180   We'd need no prompting, would we,
The girls you left behind, and their mother,
To give you the welcome you deserve.
By all the gods, don't force me
To harden my heart towards you, or to think
Thoughts that are evil. And don't force yourself
To think and do what you know to be wrong!
But . . . supposing you do sacrifice your child?
What will you ask for in your prayers, what blessings
Will you pray for, as you cut your daughter's throat?
A homecoming as filthy as your filthy departure?
And what blessings do you suppose
I should call down upon you in my prayers?
Do you imagine the gods to be idiots,
Who will reward murderers, just for the asking?
And when you finally get back to Argos,

1190   Will you open your arms and expect your children
To embrace you? You would have no right
To ask such a thing. Which of them would dare
To look you in the eye, or trust your embraces,
Knowing you killed their sister! Have you followed my
                                reasoning
So far? Have you thought this through at all?
Or is your only thought how to preserve your position
As General of the army? A real General
Would have stood up proudly among the Greeks
And spoken like a leader, with wisdom and justice,
Saying, 'Soldiers of Greece, do you really want
To sail to Phrygia? Then you must draw lots
To see whose daughter must die. That would have been
The just, the equitable thing to do,
Not picking on your own daughter

1200   As a sacrifice for the whole Greek nation!
If that's to be the case, let Menelaus
Kill his daughter, Hermione, in front of her mother.
It's his business, the whole expedition,
Not yours. But as things stand now,
I, who have been utterly chaste and faithful
To you, must watch my daughter die,

While Helen the whore, whose promiscuity
Was the only cause of this disaster
Can bring her little girl back home
To Sparta, and live in peace and prosperity!
And now, you tell me if anything I've said
Is one whit less than the plain truth.
And even if it is, for God's sake,
I beg you, don't kill our daughter.
For a sane man, there isn't any choice!

CHORUS.
To save a child's life is good morality
In anyone's language. Be persuaded, Agamemnon.   1210

IPHIGENIA.
Father, if I had Orpheus' voice
And could charm the rocks and stones to dance
To my music, I'd so ravish your ears,
With my songs, that everyone would do my bidding
Like slaves. As it is, I have no skill
In singing, no magical powers
Except the power of tears, so they
Must serve for weapons. I have no garlands
To embrace you with, only arms,
This body of mine, which my mother bore you.
Don't end my life before I've lived.
I'm too young to die yet. Life is so precious,
Even the plain daylight is so beautiful,
Don't drive me down into the darkness
Of the grave, not yet! I am the first
Of your children to call you Father, the first   1220
You called your child, the first to clamber
Up onto your knees to smother you with kisses
And be kissed in return. Do you remember
What you used to say? 'Well my little girl,
Shall I live to see you happily married
In some other man's house, living in a manner
Worthy of Agamemnon's daughter?' And then,
Remember what I said, pulling at your beard
As I stroke it now, 'What shall I do for you?'

I said, 'When you're an old man, I will take you
To *my* house, and look after you there,
1230   Because you looked after me and brought me up
In *your* house, so that makes it fair.'
I remember every word of those childish conversations;
But you must have forgotten them, if you're prepared
To kill me. No, I beg you, by our ancestor
Pelops, by your own father, Atreus,
By my mother, standing here,
Whose agony brought me into the world
And must now endure a more terrible anguish
As I go out of it. That marriage
Between Paris and Helen, what has it got to do
With me? Tell me, Father, one reason
Why that marriage should cause my death!
Look at me now, look me in the eye,
Kiss me again, so that if I die,
If you are quite hardened to persuade or reason,
1240   I shall have that at least to remember you by.
Baby brother, you're only a little boy,
You can't help those who love you yet,
But you're old enough to cry, as I'm crying,
To beg your father not to kill your sister.
The tiniest child has a sense of evil,
Even before he can speak, he recognises that
With his tears. His silence is the most eloquent persuasion.
Pity me Father. I'm young. Spare my life.
We both beg the same thing, moistening your beard
With our tears, the grown girl and the infant boy
Scarce out of the womb. One word will convince you,
1250   I know. Nothing is sweeter than sunlight,
The joy of being alive. To be dead is to be nothing,
Non-existent, in the grave. Only madmen want to die.
It's far better to live in misery
Than to die even the most glorious death.

CHORUS.
Your wickedness, Helen, that marriage, will bring misery
To the sons of Atreus, and to their children.

AGAMEMNON.
   You don't have to tell me what's pitiable
   And what's not! I love my own children,
   Only a madman doesn't! It's terrifying to me,
   Wife, listen . . . ! To be pushed to such
   Desperate extremes, but it's equally terrifying
   To refuse! I've got to do it! Look
   Around you! Do you see this massive army,   1260
   Do you see all these stationary ships
   Like a fence shutting us in,
   Do you see all this weaponry and armour,
   All the kings and leaders of the Greek army,
   Who won't get a passage across to Troy,
   Nor ever conquer those famous towers
   And terraces of the citadel, unless
   I sacrifice you. Calchas the prophet
   Says so. And there's a terrifying energy
   Like the uncontrollable power of lust
   In the Greek army, to get across
   To those barbarians, and teach them once and for all
   That they can't carry off the wives of Greece
   Without terrible retribution. And they will kill
   My two little girls in Argos, and you two,
   And me as well, if I refuse to obey
   The commands of the goddess! Do you understand?
   Menelaus hasn't forced my hand.
   My girl, I'm not doing this to please him!
   But for Greece. It's for Greece, whether I like it   1270
   Or not, you must be sacrificed.
   We're all of us under that obligation.
   Greece must be free, and as far as it lies in you
   To achieve that, so far you must go,
   And so must I too! We are all Greeks.
   We must not allow the wives of Greece
   To be ravished from their beds by barbarians!
   Exit AGAMEMNON.

CLYTEMNESTRA.
   Oh my child – and you strangers from across the bay,

How can I bear such pain? Your father sells you
As a bride for death, and then runs away!

IPHIGENIA.

The song of death for us both now, mother and daughter,
A last threnody, and we must sing it together.
1280　Fate, like a thundercloud, darkens the sky,
Never bright daylight again for me,
Never the sun's warm shining, my way
Is to darkness, and cold eternity.
O you snow-covered valley of Phrygia, and Mount Ida,
Where Priam took the baby he had dragged from its

mother

And left it alone in your forests to die,
You sheltered him, nurtured him, so that in Troy
They called him Prince Paris of Ida, the mountain shepherd
1290　　　　　　　　　　　　　　　　　　　　　　　　　boy.

And why so softly did you shelter him there,
Paris Alexander, in cattle stall
And sheepfold, like a child of nature, where
Springs rise in secret, and white streams fall,
And by the shining mirrored water
Nymphs comb their golden hair
In river meadows thick with bluebells, which goddesses

gather

For garlands such as immortals wear?

To that fated place, where Paris lay,
1300　Came Pallas Athene, one ominous day,
And dangerous Aphrodite from Cyprus, and Hera,
And Hermes, Zeus' messenger. All three –
Aphrodite, voluptuous with sex, Pallas the bearer
Of the spear of law, and Hera, she
Who shares the bed of Zeus, determined to play
The bitter game of beauty, and bear away
The prize that will breed bloodshed and horror,
1310　And bring death for me, my death,
For a promise of immortal fame, and a few feet of earth.

This sacrifice, my life, Artemis demands,
My blood must launch the ships for Troy.

O Mother, my mother, my father commands
My obedience, betrays me, then runs away,
Leaving me defenceless. My bitterest curse,
All bitterness, on Helen, and the fate that binds
My life to expiate her sin – what could be worse? –
Murdered by a father's sacrilegious hands!

Oh why did the bronze-beaked ships come here
With their oars of slender pine, to be beached on the
                                                    shore   1320
Of Aulis, on their way to Troy?
And why did Zeus send a contrary wind
Against our fleet, while he smoothes the way
For other sailors? Who knows the mind
Of a god, who makes the sailing fair
For some men and blows others to despair,
Fills some ships' sails till they bulge with joy,
Slack canvas for others, breezes abating   1330
To a dead calm, and the misery of waiting?

So many agonies, so much suffering
Mortal men inherit.
Our term is fixed, terror our ending,
None can escape it.
But never greater agony, never more terrible slaughter
Inflicted on the sons of Greece, than by Helen, Tyndareus'
                                                    daughter!

CHORUS.
   I pity you, child. In your short life, nothing
   Could deserve such bad luck, such injustice, such
                                                    an ending.

IPHIGENIA.
   Mother, there's a crowd of men, running this way!

CLYTEMNESTRA.
   It's him. The man you came for! Thetis' son.

IPHIGENIA.
   Women, open the doors, let me hide my face . . .   1340

CLYTEMNESTRA.
   Don't hide.

IPHIGENIA.
> I can't look at Achilles without blushing.

CLYTEMNESTRA.
Why not?

IPHIGENIA.
> That sham marriage! I'm too ashamed!

CLYTEMNESTRA.
You're in no position to be fastidious.
Swallow your pride, girl, it's your last chance.

Enter ACHILLES.

ACHILLES.
Unhappy child of Leda.

CLYTEMNESTRA.
> You call me my true name.

ACHILLES.
There's a riot in the army.

CLYTEMNESTRA.
> They're shouting. What about?

ACHILLES.
It's your daughter, they're saying . . .

CLYTEMNESTRA.
> God help us, what?

ACHILLES.
That she must be killed.

CLYTEMNESTRA.
> And does no one speak for her?

ACHILLES.
I got into a fight myself . . .

CLYTEMNESTRA.
> My dear friend, what fight?

ACHILLES.
The real thing. They stoned me.

CLYTEMNESTRA.
1350
> Because you tried to save her?

ACHILLES.
   That's right.

CLYTEMNESTRA.
                    And who dared to lay hands on you?

ACHILLES.
   The whole bloody army!

CLYTEMNESTRA.
                    Weren't the Myrmidons there?

ACHILLES.
   They threw the first stones!

CLYTEMNESTRA.
                    My darling, it's the end . . .

ACHILLES.
   I've been bought off by marriage, they said.

CLYTEMNESTRA.
                    Did you answer?

ACHILLES.
   Said, don't you lay a finger on my wife!

CLYTEMNESTRA.
                    That's right!

ACHILLES.
   Said her father promised her.

CLYTEMNESTRA.
                    Had her brought here from Argos.

ACHILLES.
   But they shouted me down.

CLYTEMNESTRA.
                    Uncivilised rabble!

ACHILLES.
   But I'll fight them for you still.

CLYTEMNESTRA.
                    One man against an army.

ACHILLES.
   See these chaps with my armour . . . ?

CLYTEMNESTRA.

God bless you for your courage!

ACHILLES.

The whole world will bless me!

CLYTEMNESTRA.

1360   Who dares sacrifice her now?

ACHILLES.

No one, while I live.

CLYTEMNESTRA.

Will they come for her by force?

ACHILLES.

Thousands of them, Odysseus in command.

CLYTEMNESTRA.

Of Sisyphus' family?

ACHILLES.

That's the one.

CLYTEMNESTRA.

Was he elected, or did he choose himself?

ACHILLES.

Elected, but it was fixed.

CLYTEMNESTRA.

Filthy choice! Child murderer!

ACHILLES.

Don't worry, I'll stop him!

CLYTEMNESTRA.

Will he drag her away?

ACHILLES.

Right first time. By her golden hair!

CLYTEMNESTRA.

What shall I do?

ACHILLES.

Hang on to her tight!

CLYTEMNESTRA.

My bare arms will protect her.

ACHILLES.
  It may come to that . . .

IPHIGENIA.
                    Mother, listen to me!
Don't be angry with your husband, that's pointless now.
No one can easily bear what's unbearable.   1370
Achilles deserves our thanks for trying to help us,
But we mustn't let him destroy his position
In the army, and maybe lose his life
For our sakes, and to no purpose.
That will be a disaster for him,
And won't save us. Listen Mother,
Let me tell you what I think . . . I must die . . .
That has suddenly become very clear to me.
And if I must die, let me do it decently,
With dignity and courage . . . No, no Mother,
You can't deny what I'm saying, if you look at it
My way, you'll know I'm right!
What nation is greater than Greece? And all
The Greeks now look to me for an answer,
Everything depends on me, the safe passage
Of the invasion fleet, the destruction of Troy,
And safety, in the future, for all Greek wives
From abduction by foreigners. No woman again   1380
Will ever be dragged from her home and contentment
By force, when the whole world will have seen
The price Paris will pay for the rape of Helen!
I shall achieve all that at a stroke, simply
By giving my life. I shall become famous
As the woman who set Greece free . . .
So why should I hang on to life so desperately?
When you gave me birth, Mother, it was as a Greek woman,
Part of the Greek nation, not just for yourself.
There are ten thousand men here, armed to the teeth,
Another ten thousand stripped at the oars
Ready to row – and why? Because
Their fatherland, the beloved country,
Has been wronged, and insulted, and for its sake

They-will dare anything, however dangerous
Against their enemies, and die for Greece
If need be. How can my single life
1390   Stand against that? How could that be right?
How could it be just? Could I say one word
In my own defence? What arguments could I use?
And there's one thing more. Why should Achilles
Take on the whole Greek army single handed,
And probably be killed, for the sake of a woman?
What use are women in war? One brave man
Is worth ten thousand of us. And if Artemis,
Being a great goddess, demands my body,
Who am I, a mere mortal, to oppose her wishes?
That's out of the question. I dedicate my body
As a gift for Greece. Take me. Sacrifice me.
And then to Troy, plunder the whole city,
When you leave it, leave a ruin! That will be
My memorial. A Greek victory
Will be the marriage I never celebrated,
The children I never bore, a name
Remembered through the generations!
1400   It is Greek destiny, Mother, to rule barbarians:
Barbarians must never rule Greeks.
Why? Because they are born slaves,
And for Greeks, freedom is our birthright!

CHORUS.

The young girl is a model of nobility. But there's something
Evil in a goddess that demands such sacrifices.

ACHILLES.

Daughter of Agamemnon, what a blessing
It would have been, if the gods had allowed me
To win you for my wife. I envy Greece,
Whose bride you now become, and I envy you too
For giving your body for Greece. Everything
You said was admirable, memorably expressed,
And worthy of your fatherland. You have decided
Not to fight the gods, they are too powerful.
You have faced the inevitable by doing the wise

And the correct thing. Such strength of character
Only increases my passionate desire   1410
To have you for my wife. You're a remarkable woman,
And worthy of your country. Now listen to me.
I want to do everything I can to help you.
For the chance of taking you home with me
I'd dare anything. And – by Thetis, my mother,
I swear it! – I'm angry and disappointed
Not to be able to save you, even if
That means fighting the whole Greek army!
Think for a moment. It's a dreadful thing to die.

IPHIGENIA.
No, listen to me. I have no hope now,
And no fear either. They mean nothing anymore.
It's bad enough that Helen's body
Should cause men to fight and kill each other.
You mustn't die, my friend, nor kill anyone
On my account. So, leave me now.
Let me save Greece, if it's in my power to do it.   1420

ACHILLES.
What courage, what greatness of spirit!
What can I say to such resolution?
Let me speak the plain truth, and call you
A superior being, an aristocratic soul!
Nevertheless, it is possible you might regret
What you said in the heat of the moment, and want
To change your mind, so listen carefully
To what I'm saying. I shall place my weapons
Right next to the altar! Fully prepared
Not to allow them to kill you. To stop them
By force, if necessary! It may be
That even you, when the knife is at your throat,
Will see things differently, and remember my promise.
You won't lose your life for a momentary impulse   1430
Afterwards regretted. Not in my presence!
I shall go now, taking my weapons with me,
To the sanctuary of the goddess Artemis. I shall stand
Right by the altar; and wait there, till you come.

Exit ACHILLES *as* PRIESTESSES *enter to prepare*
IPHIGENIA *for sacrifice.*

IPHIGENIA.
No sound, Mother, but tears. Why are you crying?

CLYTEMNESTRA.
I have some cause to cry. My heart is broken.

IPHIGENIA.
I'll be frightened if you cry. Do one thing for me . . .

CLYTEMNESTRA.
What is it? Whatever, I can't refuse.

IPHIGENIA.
Don't wear black for me, or cut off your hair.

CLYTEMNESTRA.
How can you ask that? When I've lost my daughter . . .

IPHIGENIA.
No Mother, not lost. Remembered for ever.

CLYTEMNESTRA.
1440   What do you mean? When I've lost you, I must grieve . . .

IPHIGENIA.
Why should you grieve? There won't be any grave.

CLYTEMNESTRA.
It's not the grave, it's the death people grieve for.

IPHIGENIA.
My tomb will be the altar of Artemis, Zeus' daughter.

CLYTEMNESTRA.
I'll do what you ask child. I know you must be right . . .

IPHIGENIA.
I'm the lucky one. To give all I have for Greece!

CLYTEMNESTRA.
And your sisters, what message shall I give to them?

IPHIGENIA.
That they must never wear black for me either.

CLYTEMNESTRA.
But something personal . . . some loving word.

IPHIGENIA.
Just say . . . 'Goodbye'. Tell Orestes to be a man.   1450

CLYTEMNESTRA.
Cuddle him close then. You'll never see him again . . .

IPHIGENIA.
My little darling . . . you did all you could, didn't you?

CLYTEMNESTRA.
Can I do anything for you, when I get back home?

IPHIGENIA.
Yes. Don't hate my father. Remember he's your husband.

CLYTEMNESTRA.
He's running his own race now. Against terror.

IPHIGENIA.
He doesn't want to kill me. He's doing it for Greece.

CLYTEMNESTRA.
It's a disgusting sham! His ancestors would disown him.

IPHIGENIA.
Who will escort me . . . ? They'll hold my head back, .
                                         by the hair.

CLYTEMNESTRA.
I'll come with you . . .

IPHIGENIA.
                  No Mother, that wouldn't be right.

CLYTEMNESTRA.
I'll hang on to your clothes . . . !

IPHIGENIA.
                  No Mother, believe me!   1460
Stay here. It will be better that way
For both of us. My father's guards, please,
Let one of them escort me to the garden
Of Artemis, where I am to be slaughtered.

CLYTEMNESTRA.
  My child, you're going . . . !
IPHIGENIA.

                                And I shall never return.

CLYTEMNESTRA.
  Leaving me, I'm your mother . . .
IPHIGENIA.

                            We don't deserve this, do we?

CLYTEMNESTRA.
  Don't go, wait a moment . . .
IPHIGENIA.

                              Not one tear Mother. Not one!

The PRIESTESSES *come forward, and begin to prepare*
  IPHIGENIA.

IPHIGENIA.
  Women, sing a hymn for me, chant of my fate
  In honour of Artemis, the daughter of Zeus.
  Let all the sons of Greece throughout the camp
  Be silent. This moment is holy. Let the priests
1470   Prepare the instruments of sacrifice.
  Sprinkle the barley to purify the flames,
  And let my father begin to circle the altar,
  Always to the right, according to the ritual.
  My sacrifice brings salvation to the Greeks, and victory!
  Lead me now, Troy's destroyer,
  The Phrygian people's despair,
  Crown me with flowers, bind me with garlands,
  Set blossoms like jewels in my hair;
  Wash my hands in the ewers of holy water
  And dance to Artemis, link hands
1480   In circles round the shrine
  To where her altar stands.
  All honour to the goddess. This blood of mine
  Will cancel the gods' decree
  And the ships will put to sea.
  Oh Mother, dear Mother, my eyes
  Flow like fountains for you here.

They must be dry at the altar. Sing,   1490
Women, from the temple, where
It faces across the straits to where Chalcis lies.
At Aulis, the crowded harbours ring
With the shouts of soldiers, fired
For war, a forest of weapons waving,
By my name alone inspired.
Glory to the fatherland! I shall never
See Mycenae again. Goodbye, for ever!   1500

CHORUS.

Do you praise the Cyclops' masterpiece
The stones their hands laid, Perseus' city?

IPHIGENIA.

That city bred me to be a beacon for Greece.
I give Greece my life now, give it willingly.

CHORUS.

Your glory will shine through eternity.

IPHIGENIA.

Goodbye, daylight.
Great torch of the world, goodbye.
Another life for me now, another time
All unknown and strange, my eternal home.
Goodbye, daylight,
For ever, for ever, goodbye.

Exeunt IPHIGENIA *and* PRIESTESSES.

CHORUS.

See where she goes now, Troy's destroyer,   1510
To bring Phrygians to despair.
Clusters of flowers weaved in garlands
For death in her golden hair,
Veiled in the purity of holy water,
To where the fearful altar stands
Of the bloodthirsty goddess, to offer
For the blood sacrifice she demands
Her own white throat, and suffer
The gash of the knife, and flood
The altar with sacrificial blood.

Your father waits there, he fills the bowl
With wine and pure water.
The whole Greek army is assembled, burning
1520   To begin the Trojan slaughter.
Grant us luck, Queen Artemis, to achieve that goal.
Great lady, we've satisfied your ancient yearning
For blood. Launch our expedition
Against Phrygia, and Trojan cunning.
And may the greatest soldier of the Greek nation,
Agamemnon, end the story
1530   Crowned with immortal glory.

Enter a MESSENGER.

MESSENGER.
Clytemnestra, Tyndareus' daughter! If you're inside
The headquarters, come out! I've something extraordinary
                                                    to tell you!

Enter CLYTEMNESTRA.

CLYTEMNESTRA.
I heard you shouting, and came out at once.
Something in your voice made me shudder with terror.
Can there be greater disasters than I already endure?
There can be nothing worse.

MESSENGER.
                           It's your daughter.
Something happened. It was awesome . . . wonderful!

CLYTEMNESTRA.
Then tell me, quickly. Don't hold anything back!

MESSENGER.
1540   My dear mistress, not a word, I'll tell you everything
Right from the beginning – though my mind's confused
Still, my tongue might garble it a bit.
When we came to the sacred grove
And the gardens thick with flowers where Artemis'
                                                    sanctuary
Stands, we found the whole Greek army on parade
There, all pressing forward, and eager to see everything.
And when Agamemnon saw his daughter

Entering the temple precinct, correctly prepared
As a sacrificial victim, he cried out, aloud,
In terrible pain; then tried to turn his head away
From her, and from the army, and wept like a child,
Hiding his face in his cloak. She came   1550
Close enough to touch him, this man who was her father,
And said this, or something like it:
'Here I am, Father, as you commanded me,
Ready to play my part. I give my body
For the sake of my country, and all the nations
Of the Greeks, most willingly. Take me by the hand
To the altar. Sacrifice me there, if that
Is what the goddess requires. I wish
You luck, and insofar as it lies in me
To influence a goddess, all prosperity.
May you win the great prize of victory,
And return in triumph to your fatherland.
But because I come willingly, please
Don't let any of the Greeks touch me.
I won't make a noise, and I'll stretch my neck
                                           forward   1560
Without any fear.' Everyone present
Was immensely impressed at this young girl's
Extraordinary courage, and her decorum,
Her sense of what was right. Then Talthybius,
Whose duty it was, stepped forward, and called aloud
To the army that speaking was utterly forbidden,
And that each man should observe a reverent silence.
The Priest Calchas drew the knife from its sheath –
So sharp it almost cut you to look at it,
Placed it on a golden dish, and crowned
The girl's head with flowers. Then Peleus' son,
Achilles, took the golden dish, sprinkled it
With holy water from the vessels, then
Solemnly bearing it around the altar,
Uttered this prayer. 'Daughter of Zeus,   1570
Artemis the hunter, thirsty for the blood
Of wild animals, moon goddess,
Bright light wheeling in the dark heavens,

Receive this sacrifice we offer,
The whole Greek army, and its leader, Agamemnon,
The pure blood from the white neck
Of an innocent virgin. Grant us in return
A fair wind and good passage for our ships
To Troy, and that we may storm the city
And overwhelm the citadel by the force of our arms.'
The two brothers, the sons of Atreus,
Stood there, eyes down, staring at the ground,
And the whole army followed suit.
Then the priest lifted up the knife,
Said a short prayer over the girl
And took level aim at her throat, ready
To cut it. And I can tell you,
As I stood there with my head down,
1580 I was sick to the stomach, I could feel the pain
In my own heart. Then suddenly . . .
Something wonderful happened. I can only call it a miracle.
We all heard the knife strike her throat
Horribly clearly, but . . . there was no girl
Stretched out on the ground where we expected her to be!
Calchas suddenly shouted out, and the whole army
Cried out in amazement, like an echo,
Seeing before their eyes what was clearly
The visible hand of the gods, something
We couldn't believe, even though it was there
Before our eyes. What lay gasping
Its life out on the ground, and flooding the altar
With its blood, was a deer, a large one too,
1590 Worthy of a goddess. Calchas spoke up
At once, with what joy in his voice you can imagine,
'Leaders of the Greek army, feast
Your eyes on this sacrifice, which the goddess
Herself offers on the altar, a deer
Bred to run like the wind on the mountains.
This is a sacrifice she welcomes, prefers
Even, before the girl, not wanting to stain
Her altar with the blood of a virgin
So noble, both in her birth and her actions.

This is an offering she delights in,
And she grants us in return a fair wind
And a fast passage to sweep down upon Troy!
So let every soldier and sailor now
Summon up his courage, and return to his ship
And be ready to embark this very day,
Leaving these safe harbours here at Aulis   1600
To launch into the long swell of the Aegean!'
Then, when the whole sacrifice had burned to ashes
On the altar in the sacrificial flame,
He made the customary prayer for a good
Passage and safe return for the army . . .
And Agamemnon sent me to tell you the news,
And, particularly, to emphasise what a marvellous favour
He has received from the gods, and how it confers
On him imperishable glory among the Greeks.
I was there, and I'm telling you what happened
Exactly as I saw it, with my own eyes!
The girl, quite obviously, has been transported
Up to the heavens, to live among the gods.
So you can put an end to all your grief
For her, and there is no cause at all   1610
For anger towards your husband. Divine
Intervention into the affairs of men
Is always unexpected, and those whom the gods
Especially love, they'll save, some way or another.
In one day you have seen your daughter's death
And rebirth, darkness transformed into light.

CHORUS.
   Could any messenger bring happier news?
   Your daughter is alive, living among the gods!

CLYTEMNESTRA.
   My dear child, which of the gods
   Came like a thief and robbed me of my treasure?
   How shall I think of you, or speak of you now?
   Shall I pray to heaven, or weep to earth?
   And you, Captain. Do you expect me to believe this story?

Isn't it a lie, concocted for my benefit,
To soothe me and keep me quiet?
You bring me plasters for a broken heart.

CHORUS.
Here comes the Lord Agamemnon. He'll tell you
1620   The same story, I'm sure, and understand what it means.

Enter AGAMEMNON.

AGAMEMNON.
Wife. Everyone will envy how our marriage has been
                                          blessed
With our eldest daughter. She is one of the company
Of the gods, of that there is no question.
Your duty now is to take good care
Of that little soldier of mine, and go back home.
The army, as you can see, is ready to embark,
And it may be some considerable time
Before I return and pay my respects to you
In person. I hope things go well with you.

CHORUS.
Make your journey, son of Atreus, with joy
To the land of Phrygia, and joyfully return
Loaded with the treasure of plundered Troy!

Exeunt AGAMEMNON, CLYTEMNESTRA *and*
CHORUS.

CYCLOPS

translated by J Michael Walton

Characters

SILENUS, an old man, father of the Satyrs
ODYSSEUS, King of Ithaca
CYCLOPS, the one-eyed giant Polyphemus
CHORUS of Satyrs
CREWMEN of Odysseus

Enter SILENUS.

SILENUS.

Dionysus! It's your fault I'm still as full of aches and pains
as when I had a young man's body. Hera drove you crazy
then and you ran off, abandoning your nurses, the mountain-
nymphs. That was the first time. Then when I stood at your
side, your companion-in-arms, in the battle with the earth-
born giants: what a time that was. You remember, I
smashed Enceladus right through the skull with my spear.
Killed him, stone dead. What do you mean, I dreamt it? It
wasn't a dream when I showed Dionysus the spoils. He'll
take some bailing out this time, though. Listen. It was
Hera again. She persuaded a gang of Tuscan pirates   10
to take you on an extended sea-voyage, didn't she? As
soon as I heard about it, I set sail with the lads to rescue
you. There I stood at the helm, guiding the ship, while my
boys strained at the oars, churning the blue sea white. We
were looking for you, Lord. We hadn't quite reached Malea
– we were close – when an east wind blew up and drove us
onto the rocky shore of Etna where the sons of Neptune   20
live, the Cyclopes, one-eyed cave-dwellers, man-eaters.

One of them captured us and forced us to become his
slaves. The master we now serve is known as Polyphemus.
No more Bacchic junketings for us. We are shepherds for
this godless creature. They are down there now, my lads,
no, over there at the foot of the mountain, minding the
sheep. So young, poor things. My lads, that is, not the
sheep. I stay here to top up the troughs and clean up his   30
quarters and serve his Stygian stews. I must go and rake
out all his filth ready to welcome them back, my master and
his sheep.

There are my boys now. I can see them, driving the sheep.
No, over there. Hey, what are they up to? What's that
clapping noise? I don't believe it. They're dancing. They're
dancing the *sikinnis*. It's like being back at Althea's house
dancing for Dionysus, playing, singing, camping about
and I don't know what else.   40

Enter CHORUS *with sheep*.

CHORUS.

Get down here.
Your fathers were of high degree,
Your mothers have a pedigree.
D'you hear?

What's the rush?
Why're you heading for the heights,
When you'll find your grazing rights
Are just as lush

By the trough,
Where the breeze is fast asleep
50   And the water's running deep
For you to quaff?

Accursed flock!
While your desperate lambs are bleating
You can only think of eating.
Here's a rock,

Here's a brick.
Get down here, you brood of Cyclops
Or you'll get it in the lamb-chops
Double-quick.

Hear them bleat.
60   Little lambs left in the fold
By evening need a sucking-hold
Nose to teat.

Do it now.
You need milking. They need feeding,
They've been sleeping. You're not heeding.
You know how.

Come away
To your cave in Etna's deep.
The best grass will always keep
Another day.

So sad.
No more Bacchus, no more dances,

No more thyrsus-waving Bacchants.
No more cymbals' rowdy clash;
No more happy wine-jars' splash;
No more nymphs in headlong rush;
Where the springing fountains gush.
Too bad.

I call on Dionysus.
I sing to Aphrodite.   70
I hunt her 'midst the bare-foot Bacchants.
Where do you wander, my Dionysus?
Where do you shake your golden hair?
I serve Polyphemus.
I attend the one-eyed Cyclops.
I slave for him, tricked out in filthy goatskin.
Where do you wander, my Dionysus?
Starved of your love,   80
I would that I were there.

SILENUS.
Shush, lads. That's enough. Get the attendants to shut the
sheep in the shelter.

CHORUS.
Off you go now. Shoo. What's all the rush, father?

SILENUS.
I can see a boat on the shore. And it's Greek. Lords of the
oar, there on the shore. No, they're heading this way. And
they've got their commander with them. What's that they're
carrying? It looks like baskets. Empty baskets and pitchers.
They're after supplies. Poor things. Whoever they are,   90
they can't know who Polyphemus is, nor what sort of
reception they'll get, or they wouldn't be heading for this
cannibal cave. Quiet now, quiet. Let's at least find out
who they are and how they happen to be in Sicily.

Enter ODYSSEUS *and his men.*

ODYSSEUS.
Strangers, friends. Do you have any running water round
here? We're a little bit parched, I can't deny it. And I don't
suppose there's anyone with a bite or two to spare. We'll

pay, naturally. Aye, aye, what's all this? It looks as though
we've happened in on the garden-city of Dionysus. Those
are satyrs, that crowd over there by the cave. I'll address
myself to the decrepit one. Hello, old man.

SILENUS.
Welcome, strangers. Who are you? Where do you come
from?

ODYSSEUS.
I am Odysseus. King of the Cephallenians. Odysseus, from
Ithaca.

SILENUS.
I've heard of you. Son of Sisyphus and a right rattle.

ODYSSEUS.
That's who I am. So less of the lip.

SILENUS.
Where did you set out for Sicily from?

ODYSSEUS.
From Troy. We've come from the Trojan War.

SILENUS.
Troy? You can't be much of a navigator if you're heading
for Ithaca.

ODYSSEUS.
A force ten gale drove us here.

SILENUS.
Hard luck. The same thing happened to me.

ODYSSEUS.
Then you too were driven here unwillingly?

SILENUS.
We were chasing pirates who had kidnapped Dionysus.

ODYSSEUS.
What place is this? Does anyone live here?

SILENUS.
That mountain there, that's Etna, highest in Sicily.

ODYSSEUS.
There's no sign of walls or fortifications, as far as I can see.
Is there a city near here?

SILENUS.
No. No people, so no city.

ODYSSEUS.
Who does the land belong to? Or is it the province of the
wild beast?

SILENUS.
Cyclopes. And they don't live in houses. They live in caves.

ODYSSEUS.
Do they obey one man? Or do they favour democracy?

SILENUS.
They're a solitary lot. There's none of them pays no
attention to nobody.   120

ODYSSEUS.
A predominantly cereal-crop economy, I imagine. How else
would they live?

SILENUS.
Milk, cheese and mutton.

ODYSSEUS.
And they cultivate Dionysus, eh? Fruit of the vine?

SILENUS.
Not a drop. It's a rotten place. No drinking, no dancing.

ODYSSEUS.
A decent welcome for strangers, though, I expect?

SILENUS.
If they're juicy. They eat them.

ODYSSEUS.
Eat them? Do you mean they feast on human flesh?

SILENUS.
Yes, they eat them. Allcomers.

ODYSSEUS.
Where is this Cyclops? He's not in there, is he?

SILENUS.

130   He's out hunting on Etna with the dogs.

ODYSSEUS.

We'd better get a move on. Do us a favour.

SILENUS.

I don't know about that, Odysseus. Of course we'd like to help.

ODYSSEUS.

Sell us some bread. We've nothing left.

SILENUS.

Like I told you, there's only meat.

ODYSSEUS.

Only meat? Fine. Beggars can't be choosers.

SILENUS.

Cheese, we got, fig-juice, cheese and milk.

ODYSSEUS.

Fetch it out. We want to see what we're buying.

SILENUS.

How much have you got? In gold?

ODYSSEUS.

We don't actually have any gold. We do have a rather special vintage . . .

SILENUS.

Wine? Oh, bless you, sir, bless you. That's been in short
140   supply round here.

ODYSSEUS.

And this is rather special, as I said. A present from Dionysus' own son, Maron.

SILENUS.

Maron? Not Maron. Why, I used to nurse him in these very arms, so I did.

ODYSSEUS.

That's the one. Son of Dionysus.

SILENUS.
It will be back on board, I suppose. You wouldn't have it with you?
ODYSSEUS.
Yes, I do. Here it is. In this wineskin.
SILENUS.
In that? That is hardly a decent mouthful.
ODYSSEUS.
More than you think and twice enough to see you under the table.
SILENUS.
You're talking liquid pleasure.
ODYSSEUS.
You fancy a drop, do you? Neat, naturally.
SILENUS.
Oh, of course. Call it a buyer's sample.   150
ODYSSEUS.
The flask comes with matching accessory. Have a cup.
SILENUS.
Oh, that takes me back.
ODYSSEUS.
There, now.
SILENUS.
Oh, I say. Oh my. What a bouquet.
ODYSSEUS.
Take a look at that.
SILENUS.
It's a sniff of it I want.
ODYSSEUS.
Enough of this talk. What about a taste?
SILENUS.
Yes. Mmmm, yes. Feet, Dionysus says you gotta dance. Da, da, dee. Da, da, da.
ODYSSEUS.
And how did that lubricate your larynx?

SILENUS.
It's making my toe-nails curl.

ODYSSEUS.

160   Actually, we could offer cash.

SILENUS.
Forget the cash. Untie the skin.

ODYSSEUS.
We'll need some cheeses then. And a few lambs.

SILENUS.
Anything, anything. What's a Cyclops matter? Just one
more mouthful or I'll go crazy. You can buy the flock, the
whole lot, and I'll go and jump in the sea off the Leucadian
Rock, so long as I can get tanked up to the eyeballs first.
Anyone who doesn't like drinking must be . . . must be out
of his mind. With a drink inside you, you can face the

170   world, erect, grab yourself a fistful of tit and let your hands
roam free over some of those soft acres. Bit of dancing.
Begone dull care. Give me one more slurp at the skin and
I'll tell that big, dumb Cyclops what he can do with his eye-
socket.

CHORUS.
Here, Odysseus. Can we have a word?

ODYSSEUS.
Fire away. We are all friends here.

CHORUS.
Did you really capture Troy?

ODYSSEUS.
Certainly.

CHORUS.
And get Helen back?

ODYSSEUS.
We sacked Priam's entire domain.

CHORUS.
And when you got her, did you all give her a bang? Did
you? Give her what she wanted? I bet she enjoyed it, did

180   she? The bitch. One look at some fancy trousers and a gold

medallion and, phht. 'Bye, 'bye, Menelaus. Poor little chap.
They ought to abolish women, the whole lot of them. But
leave a few for me.

SILENUS.

Oy, Odysseus. Here's your little lambs. Pick of the flock. A
little bit of curd and a nice piece of cheese. Now, push   190
off as quick as you like. Only leave me that luscious liquor.
Oh lord, the Cyclops is coming. What are we going to do?

ODYSSEUS.

I think we're in trouble, old chap. Where can we run to?

SILENUS.

Get in the cave. You can hide there.

ODYSSEUS.

That's a terrible idea. We'd be trapped.

SILENUS.

It's not a terrible idea. There are plenty of hiding-places in
there.

ODYSSEUS.

Hide? Never. Defeated Troy would weep to see me flee a
single man. I who faced a thousand Trojans in the field. 200

If we should win, we gain eternal fame.
If die, at least we know we saved our name.

Enter CYCLOPS.

CYCLOPS.

Come on, shift yourselves. What's going on? You're not on
your holidays. This all looks a bit Bacchic, a bit Dionysiac,
to me. We'll have no Dionysus here, thanks very much.
None of your ding-dongs and your rat-a-tat tats. How's my
little lambs in the cave? Having a proper suckle? Are they
snuggling up under their mothers like they should? Is there
a full complement of cheeses in the wicker? Speak up. What
do you say? Quick, or it'll be club and tears time. Head
up. Don't look down.   210

CHORUS.

Right. Anything you say. We're looking up into the sky.
Good heavens, stars. And Orion's belt.

CYCLOPS.
  What's for breakfast?

CHORUS.
  Here it is. I hope your taste-buds are primed.

CYCLOPS.
  Are the milk churns full?

CHORUS.
  You can drink a bucketful if you want.

CYCLOPS.
  Sheeps' milk or cows', or half and half?

CHORUS.
  Please yourself. Just don't swallow me.

CYCLOPS.
220 Not likely. It would polish me off, a tum full of tap-
  dancers. Hallo, what's this posse at the door? Has the
  county been overrun with crooks and cutthroats? Those are
  my sheep, from my cave. I can see them. All hobbled for
  off. Cheese presses. And the old fellow with his meat beaten
  by the looks of him.

SILENUS.
  Oh, the pain. They murdered me. Oh, it does hurt.

CYCLOPS.
  Who murdered you? Who punched your head in, old man?

SILENUS.
230 It was them, Cyclops, when I tried to stop them robbing
  you.

CYCLOPS.
  Did they not know that I am a god? Like my father before
  me.

SILENUS.
  I did tell them, naturally. They grabbed your stuff anyway,
  ate your cheese. And they were just making off with those
  lambs over there. There was nothing I could do. They said
  they'd put you in a pillory three yards high. And extract
  your entrails through your eye-socket. And give your back a
  good flaying. And tie you up to the rowing-bench on their

ship and sell you off as a navvy or labour for the treadmill.
That sort of thing.   240

CYCLOPS.

Is that a fact? Right. Be so good as to go and sharpen the
cleavers and the carvers and get a nice big fire going. Then I
can slit their throats and barbecue the best bits to take the
edge off my appetite. Stew the rest. I'm fed up with
mountain-meat. And, if I ever have to face boiled lion again
. . . or stag . . . Time for man-chop.

SILENUS.

That's the ticket, master. Be adventurous. The old   250
menu's so boring. It's a while since we've had visitors at
this establishment.

ODYSSEUS.

Ah, Cyclops. Our turn, I think, for a few words. We
arrived here at your cave from our ship, in need of food,
which we fully intend to pay for. This individual did, in
actual fact, barter these lambs in exchange for some wine.
He was agreeable. We were agreeable. There was no
question of coercion. There's not one grain of truth in what
he says. What has happened is that he has been caught
out trading your belongings.   260

SILENUS.

Who me? You'll rot in hell, you will.

ODYSSEUS.

Only if I lie.

SILENUS.

Oh Cyclops, I swear to you, by your father Poseidon, by
Triton, by Nereus and his daughters. And by Calypso. By
the sacred waves of the sea and all the little fishes, dear
handsome Cyclops, old friend, boss, what can I say? Would
I sell your stuff? Let my lads come to a bad end if I tell a
lie. And you know how much I love them.

CHORUS.

Hold on. Hold on. I saw you selling the stuff to the   270
strangers. And if I tell a lie, let my father come to a bad
end. There's no need to harm the strangers.

CYCLOPS.
I don't believe you. I trust him more than I'd trust
Rhadamanthus. So he's right. And I've got a few words for
the strangers. Where are you from? Where do you belong?
Where were you brought up?

ODYSSEUS.
We're Ithacans by race, but we come from Troy. We were
driven here, Cyclops, by contrary winds on the way home
from sacking the city.

CYCLOPS.
Oh, you are, are you? You're the ones who trooped off to
Troy beside Scamander after that dreadful Helen.

ODYSSEUS.
That's us. A brave bunch for a doughty deed.

CYCLOPS.
280   A bad business all round. Phrygia laid to waste and all for
the sake of one woman.

ODYSSEUS.
God's will, you know. No blame attached to mortals. Be
that as it may, most noble son of the sea-god, we do throw
ourselves on your mercy, speaking as free men. Do not risk
killing these men who have come to your home as friends
and don't have them served up for lunch. It would not be
seemly. At the far corners of the Greek world we have
290   protected your father's holy places. The haven of holy
Taenarus remains inviolate. The caves on Malea's Cape:
silvery rock of sacred Athene at Sunium: sanctuaries at
Geraestus; all safe and down to us. We never gave anything
Greek to the Trojans – what a suggestion. We're in this
together, you and us. This is part of Greece, here beneath
Etna with its fire-breathing rock. And, if you respect these
arguments, the moral law – bear with me, please – decrees
that you should receive suppliants and seafarers in trouble,
300   give them presents and clothe them, not push an ox-spit up
them and kebab them for breakfast. Hasn't Priam's land
bereaved poor Greece enough, draining the blood of war-
torn corpses, robbing wives and silver-haired parents of

husbands and favourite sons? If you're going to consume
the left-overs for dessert, where can anyone turn? Hear
me, Cyclops. Restrain those greedy molars. Choose the
decent way, not this. Plenty of men have come to regret 310
short-term gain.

SILENUS.
Take my advice, Cyclops. Don't leave a scrap of him.
Swallow his tongue, then you'll become as big a bull-shitter
as he is.

CYCLOPS.
Listen, pygmy. The clever man's god is money. Everything
else is wind and words. That stuff about my father's shrines
up and down the coast, forget it. All these words, who
needs them? I'm not afraid of any thunderbolt from
Zeus, friend, 'cos I've got no reason to believe he's any 320
bigger a god than I am. And *I don't care*. About
anything. If it's raining, I go indoors where it's nice and
sheltered. If I've an appetite, I serve it, a little bit of tasty,
wild jor tame. I lounge about massaging my belly, drinking
milk by the gallon. And if Zeus thunders at me, I wank in
his face. When the north wind brings snow from up in
Thrace, I put on a fur-coat and stoke up the fire. Winter
doesn't bother me. The earth provides the grass to 330
feed my flocks – she can't help it. And I don't make a
sacrifice to anybody – except me. The biggest of my gods is
my stomach. Eat lots and drink lots every day, that's Zeus
for the discerning, and no problem. And all those who want to
decorate man's life with morals, stuff 'em. No skin off
my soul if I eat you. But just in case there are rules of 340
hospitality, so as to protect myself, as it were, I can offer
you a fire and a cauldron of salty water, to boil the flesh off
your bones nicely. Now creep off in there and show a little
respect to my household god. Reverence the altar of me.

ODYSSEUS.
Woe. Alas. The pains I bore at Troy and on the sea only to be
shipwrecked against the rude and inhospitable heart of this
unruly creature. Pallas Athene, goddess born of Zeus, 350
help me now. Now, Athene, for never was my extremity

so pressing at Troy, no nor danger so profound. And you, Zeus, god of hospitality, sitting up there in the stars, take a look at this one. For, if you cannot see what's happening here, you're not much of a Zeus and that's a fact.

Exeunt ODYSSEUS, *his men and* CYCLOPS.

CHORUS.
Open up, Cyclops,
Your hungry throat, Cyclops.
Open up, Cyclops,
It's table d'hôte, Cyclops.
Stranger, grilled or in a stew,
For a gobble, gulp or chew,
While you're lounging in your coat,
360   Made of goat, Cyclops.

No thanks, Cyclops,
I'm not your guest, Cyclops.
No thanks, Cyclops,
While you digest, Cyclops,
A sacrificial feast
More fitting for a beast,
Going home, may I suggest,
Would suit me best, Cyclops.

370   On this we'll all agree, it's a pretty rotten host
Who will entertain a stranger and then serve him up on

toast.

It's the sort of boorish manners I really can't abide
Notwithstanding the free offer of a salad on the side.

Enter ODYSSEUS.

ODYSSEUS.
Oh heavens. How can I say it? How can I tell of the terrible things I saw in the cave? More like a play than real life.

CHORUS.
What is it, Odysseus? Don't tell me that wicked Cyclops has slaughtered your companions.

ODYSSEUS.
380   Two of them, anyway. He had a good look and picked out the plumpest.

CHORUS.
You poor man. Tell us what happened.

ODYSSEUS.
As soon as we had entered that rocky place, Polyphemus lit
a fire, throwing great logs from a lofty oak onto the hearth --
three wagonloads at least. On the fire he placed his bronze
cooking-pot and drew his pine-needle bed close to the
flames. Then he milked his sheep, filling a hundred-gallon
churn with the foaming liquid. Beside it he set an ivy
bowl, four foot across, but more like six foot deep; and   390
thorn-spits, burnt to a point at one end and finished
with a billhook: all Etna's sacrificial gear.

As soon as everything was ready, this hellish cook grabbed
two of my men. In a single movement he bled one of them
into the brazen pot and, holding the other by the ankle,   400
cracked open his skull on a jagged bit of wall, so his
brains spilled out. With his knife he chopped off the flesh
to bake on the fire and put the limbs into the pot to boil. It
was terrible. Tears pouring from my eyes, I approached and
waited upon him. The others, like birds, were huddled in
the recesses of the cave, white-faced.

Sated on the flesh of my companions, the Cyclops fell back
with a vast belch. Then it came to me, a heaven-sent   410
idea. I filled a cup with Maron's wine and handed it to
him with these words: 'Cyclops, son of Poseidon', I said,
'take a look at this. Such wine you find in Greece.
Dionysus' glory.' And he, though bloated with his filthy
meal, snatched it from me and drained it off without
pausing for breath. Then he lifted his hands in delight.
'Thanks,' he said, 'my dearest guest, for supplying a fine
wine for a fine meal.' When I saw he really was delighted,
I poured him some more, well aware that the wine   420
would bewilder him and set him up for the fate he
deserved. He started to sing. I just kept filling him up:
warming his cockles and filling him up. There's the Cyclops
singing away on one side, my sailors howling away on the
other, all round the cave. What a row. So I popped out
quietly to save myself and you too, if you want. Now, do

430 you or don't you want to get away from this unconscionable
creature, so that you can live your lives with the nymphs in
the halls of Dionysus? What do you say? Your father inside
says 'Yes', but he can hardly stand up from the drink and is
glued to his cup, wings flapping like a bird trapped in lime.
But you, you're young. Let's get away together and you can
go and find your Dionysus, dear old Dionysus, a far cry
from this ghastly Cyclops.

CHORUS.

Yes, oh yes, dear friend. Just to see the day when we escape
from this ogre. My poor old prick's been in retreat recently.
440 He could do with a nibble.

ODYSSEUS.

Right then. Here's my plan to avenge myself on this foul
fiend and to effect your release.

CHORUS.

Hit me with it. You could play no sweeter music in Asia
than 'Death and the Cyclops'.

ODYSSEUS.

He's got it into his head that he wants to hold a party with
his brother-Cyclopses, so delighted is he with this draught
of Dionysus.

CHORUS.

I get you. You're going to set on him when he's by himself
in the woods, or shove him over a cliff.

ODYSSEUS.

Hardly. I prefer the subtle approach.

CHORUS.

450 What then? We always heard you were the wily one.

ODYSSEUS.

I'm going to stop him holding this party by telling him that
a Cyclops shouldn't share his wine, but keep it all for
himself. Then I'll wait until he's overcome and in a
Dionysiac stupor. There's an olive-branch in there and my
intention is to sharpen it with my sword and heat it in the
fire. As soon as it is alight, I'll pick it out and plunge it into

his eye-socket. That will sizzle his vision. And, just as a
shipwright drives his drill with a double strap, I'll twirl   460
my twig in his socket and recycle the Cyclops.

CHORUS.
Oh boy, oh boy. A wild idea. We love it.

ODYSSEUS.
And then we will all climb aboard my black ship, you, my
friends and the old man, and get away from this land
double-quick.

CHORUS.
Is there any way I could give a hand, especially with the
red-hot gouging? I would like to give a hand with the   470
gouging.

ODYSSEUS.
Certainly. It's a huge brand. All hands to the plough.

CHORUS.
I can lift a hundred cartloads, so long as I get to carbonize
his eyeball, like a wasps' nest.

ODYSSEUS.
Quietly does it, now you know the plans. On the word go,
follow your leaders. I have no intention of deserting my
men by beating a retreat. Though, of course, I could,
me being outside the cave. But it wouldn't be fair for   480
me to desert my companions – we came here together
after all – just to save my own skin.

CHORUS.
After me. Me first, not you.
Don't push, what's the rush? Form a queue.
To grasp the flaming flagpole
And shove it in his eyehole
And twiddle till his brains are seeping through.

Shhh. Quiet. Here he comes.

Under the influence, singing a song.
The tune's picayune   490
And it's ever so long.
Reeling he's roused from his revelling bunk.

We'll speed his arousal
We'll teach him carousal.
By the time that we've finished he'll end up blind drunk.

Happy the man laid out with grapes in a bunch.
Happy the man engaged with a friend after lunch,
Getting happily laid.
Happy the man with a delicate girl in his bedding
Happy the man anticipating the wedding,

500   With the bridesmaid.

Enter CYCLOPS *with* SILENUS.

CYCLOPS.
La-di-da-di-da-di-da.
I'm crammed full of wine,
With feasting replete.
My tum's like a drum,
My cargo's complete.
Which reminds me I wanted to share with my fine kin
A paean Cyclopean

510   So pass me the wineskin.

CHORUS.
With eye all-inflamed he parades from the hall.
Is it me that he loves? What a fate to befall.
The bridal torch is waiting
And she's ready for the mating
Inside that juicy hall.
Preparation's almost done.
For the groom it's just begun.
His crown still needs its multi-coloured shawl.

ODYSSEUS.
Listen here, Cyclops. There's not much I don't know about

520   this Dionysiac stuff I gave you.

CYCLOPS.
Who is he, this Dionysus? Not a proper god, is he?

ODYSSEUS.
At giving mankind pleasure, he's the best.

CYCLOPS.
Oh, what a burp. Yes, very tasty.

ODYSSEUS.
  That's the god exactly. Does no harm to anyone.

CYCLOPS.
  Doesn't he mind living in a skin, being a god?

ODYSSEUS.
  Just put him in there, not a care in the world.

CYCLOPS.
  It's not right for gods to live in skins.

ODYSSEUS.
  Who cares, as long as he makes you happy? What's your
  problem with the skin?

CYCLOPS.
  I don't like wineskins. I just like what goes in them.

ODYSSEUS.
  You stay here, then, and enjoy yourself, Cyclops.   530

CYCLOPS.
  Shouldn't I offer a drop to my brothers?

ODYSSEUS.
  Keep it to yourself. That's what you'd expect from someone
  with class.

CYCLOPS.
  It would be more friendly to share it.

ODYSSEUS.
  Parties always end in fisticuffs, I'm afraid.

CYCLOPS.
  I'm so drunk, nobody could lay a finger on me.

ODYSSEUS.
  Really, old chap. Home is the place when you're paralytic.

CYCLOPS.
  It seems a bit silly not to go to a party when you've been
  drinking.

ODYSSEUS.
  No, I assure you. 'The drunk who stays at home is no fool.'

CYCLOPS.

What are we going to do, Silenus? Do you think I should stay?

SILENUS.

540   Oh, I do, Cyclops. Who needs any more drinkers?

CYCLOPS.

Well, there you go. And the ground just here is like a feather bed made of flowers.

SILENUS.

It certainly is. It's nice to have a little drink in the sun. Stretch yourself out over there.

CYCLOPS.

What are you doing putting the bowl behind me?

SILENUS.

We don't want anyone spilling it.

CYCLOPS.

We don't want anyone drinking it. Pinching it, that's what you're after. Put it here in the middle. And you there, stranger, what's your name anyway?

ODYSSEUS.

My name is Nobody. And what have you to offer me in return?

CYCLOPS.

550   Of all the lot of you, I'll eat you last.

SILENUS.

That's a great boon you've given your guest there, Cyclops.

CYCLOPS.

Oy. What are you up to? Did you have a quick swig?

SILENUS.

Not a bit of it. It just kissed me, because I'm so pretty.

CYCLOPS.

You love wine. Wine doesn't love you. So watch it.

SILENUS.

Honest to god, it's fallen in love with me.

CYCLOPS.
Pour. To the top. Give it here.

SILENUS.
Have I got the blend right? I'd better check.

CYCLOPS.
You'll be the death of me. Hand it over.

SILENUS.
No, no. Wait till I put this garland round your head – and have a quick wet in the process.

CYCLOPS.
This cup-bearer's a villain.

SILENUS.
I am not. Oh, it is sweet, isn't it? There now, you'll 560
need a wipe-down, so's you can have a proper drink.

CYCLOPS.
That's enough. My beard and moustache are both clean.

SILENUS.
You should just lean over onto your elbow, elegantly, then you drink. No. Watch me and drink like I do, or rather, like I don't.

CYCLOPS.
Ah, what are you doing?

SILENUS.
Down to the dregs. Lovely.

CYCLOPS.
Hey, stranger. You pour.

ODYSSEUS.
You'll find the wine responds to me. It knows me.

CYCLOPS.
Just pour.

ODYSSEUS.
Shut your mouth will you? I'm pouring.

CYCLOPS.
It's difficult shutting your mouth when you're drinking. 570

ODYSSEUS.

> That's right. Pick it up. Pour it down. Don't leave a drop.
> Waste not, want not.

CYCLOPS.

> Whew. What a clever little tree that vine must be.

ODYSSEUS.

> If you pour a nice big drink on top of a nice big meal, then
> your thirst will be slaked and you can have a nice little
> sleep. Leave one drop and Dionysus will desiccate you.

CYCLOPS.

> Oh wow. I nearly drowned. Unbelievable. Whoops. Heaven
> seems to be getting muddled up with the earth. There's the
580 throne of Zeus and the glory of the gods. It's divine. Shall I
> make love to the lot of you? Don't tempt me, Graces. No
> I'll make do with my Ganymede here. I'll have a better
> jiggle with him than with all the Graces put together. I'd
> rather have little boys than women any day.

SILENUS.

> I realise that you're Zeus, Cyclops, but you're not casting
> me as Ganymede, are you?

CYCLOPS.

> The one I stole from Dardanus, yes you are, by Zeus.

SILENUS.

> Oh boys, I've had it. He's going to do unmentionable things
> to me.

CYCLOPS.

> Any objections? I may be drunk, but I'm not that drunk.

SILENUS.

> Oh lord. This is going to leave a nasty taste in the mouth.

Exeunt CYCLOPS *and* SILENUS.

ODYSSEUS.

590 Right you are, sons of Dionysus, noble fellows. Your man is
> indoors. Before long, he'll vomit up the flesh out of his vile
> throat and pass out. Inside, the stake is smoking nicely, all
> set to scorch the Cyclops' eye-hole. Courage now. Be men.

CHORUS.
  Our resolve is like granite. In you go now, before our father
  gets more than he bargained for. Everything's ready out
  here.

ODYSSEUS.
  Now Hephaestus, Lord of Etna,
  Cauterise the eye   600
  Of this thy revolting neighbour
  And rid thyself of him,
  Once and for all.
  And thou, Sleep,
  Offspring of sable Night,
  Launch thyself upon this heathen creature,
  Irresistibly.
  And after our famed Trojan tribulations,
  Destroy not Odysseus and his crew
  At the hands of one who cares
  Naught for men,
  And less for gods.
  Else we must think
  That Heaven is ruled by Luck
  And Lucky Dip more powerful than the gods.

CHORUS.
  We're singing songs
  Of savage tongs
  Ready to nobble a
  Guest-gobbler.   610

  With a blazing light
  To scramble his sight
  This stock of oak
  Ready to poke.

  No time to shirk.
  Come, wine, do your work.
  Let the Cyclops rue
  Your powerful brew.

  How I miss you, Dionysus,   620
  Ivy-kissing Dionysus.

Oh let me bid farewell
To this Cyclopean hell.
Shall I ever see you more, my Dionysus,
And dwell with you in bliss, my Dionysus?

ODYSSEUS.

Quiet, for god's sake, you animals. Hush now. Shut your
faces. Don't hawk, don't spit, don't breathe, don't even
blink. On pain of rousing that devil and missing out on the
Cyclops-gouging.

CHORUS.

We're perfectly silent, holding our breath.

ODYSSEUS.

630 Let's go then. Inside and all hands to the brand. It's well
alight.

CHORUS.

Do you think you should tell us the batting order? Who
holds the stake and where for the eye-burning? So we all get
a share. Because some of us are a bit of a long way from the
door for actually pushing the flame into the eye. And I've
just turned my ankle. Funny you should say that. I think
it's broken. I was standing over there and I just felt it go.
Me too. No idea why.

ODYSSEUS.

640 Just felt it go!

CHORUS.

Oh, dust in my eye. Ash, probably.

ODYSSEUS.

You pifflers. A fine help you turned out to be.

CHORUS.

Just because I don't want to damage my back – I've got a
bad back – and have my teeth knocked out of my head,
suddenly I'm a coward. I do know a wonderful magic song
which will make the brand jump up all by itself and sear the
skull of this one-eyed son of the soil.

ODYSSEUS.

I might have known how much use you'd be. Now I know

even better. I'll have to use my trusty crew inside. If   650
you are too feeble to lend a hand, at least give them a
bit of encouragement. Sing them a song or something.

CHORUS.
That's what I'll do. We'll take the risk, but by proxy. You
do the blinding. We'll call the tune.

Exit ODYSSEUS.

CHORUS.
Twist it, be firm with it.
Give him a perm with it.
Wind it and twine it,
Try to refine it.
Now anticlockwise and just watch him squirm with it.

Exercise, exorcise. Make his eye water.   660
Pulverise, cauterise. Give him no quarter.
Miserable animal,
Man-mangling cannibal
Grind up his cornea with pestle and mortar.

CYCLOPS (*inside*).
Ahhhh. My eye's incandescent.

CHORUS.
That's music. Bravo. Sing me some more, Cyclops.

Enter CYCLOPS.

CYCLOPS.
Ahhh. I'm assaulted. I'm destroyed. But nobody's getting
out of this cave with a smile on his face. I'll stand at the
entrance and block it with my hand.

CHORUS.
What's the problem, Cyclops?

CYCLOPS.
I'm dead.

CHORUS.
You do look dreadful.   670

CYCLOPS.
I feel awful.

CHORUS.
Did you fall in the fire while you were pissed?

CYCLOPS.
Nobody's done for me.

CHORUS.
No harm done then.

CYCLOPS.
Nobody has blinded my eye.

CHORUS.
Then you can't be blind.

CYCLOPS.
Take a look, can't you?

CHORUS.
How could nobody blind you?

CYCLOPS.
It's not funny. Where is Nobody?

CHORUS.
Nowhere, Cyclops.

CYCLOPS.
That stranger. It's the stranger has done for me. Do you
follow? That rotten devil that gave me the wine to drink.

CHORUS.
It's a terrible thing though, the drink. Two falls and a
submission, soon as you like.

CYCLOPS.
Good god, they've got away. Or are you still inside?

CHORUS.
680   They're over there by the rock, sheltering in silence.

CYCLOPS.
Which side?

CHORUS.
Right.

CYCLOPS.
Oh, right. Where?

CHORUS.
  By the rock. Got them?
CYCLOPS.
  Ouf. One damn thing after another. I've split my head open.
CHORUS.
  They're getting away.
CYCLOPS.
  Where? Over here?
CHORUS.
  No. I told you.
CYCLOPS.
  Then where?
CHORUS.
  Turn round. There, now, there, by your left hand.
CYCLOPS.
  You're mocking me. I'm just a butt.
CHORUS.
  No, of course we're not. He's standing in front of you.
CYCLOPS.
  You devil you. Where are you?
ODYSSEUS.
  Out of your reach. And taking good care that Odysseus
  stays that way.   690
CYCLOPS.
  What's that? That's a different name.
ODYSSEUS.
  Yes, Odysseus. It's the name my father gave me. And
  you've paid the price for your deplorable dinner. A fine
  thing it would have been to incinerate Troy, but not avenge
  the murder of my companions.
CYCLOPS.
  I knew it. The old oracle was right. It said you would come
  from Troy and leave me blind. But you'll have to pay a
  price too. Years more drifting about at sea.   700

ODYSSEUS.
    And you can stuff all that. I've kept my word. I'm off to the
    shore to launch my ship into the Sicilian sea and aim for
    home.

CYCLOPS.
    That's what you think. I'll tear off a rock and hurl it at your
    shipmates. I'm off up the mountain through the back door
    of the cave, even if I am blind.

    Exit CYCLOPS.

CHORUS.
    We'll join you on board, Odysseus and for the rest of our
    lives, we'll serve nobody but Dionysus.

    Exeunt omnes.

A Note on the Translators and Series Editor

PETER D. ARNOTT was born and educated in England before joining the staff of the State Univeristy of Iowa in 1958. He moved to the University of Tufts in 1969 and was teaching there up to his death in 1990. Author of twenty-five books, he wrote on the theatres of France and Japan as well as on the Classical Theatre of Greece and Rome. The last of his books, *Public and Performance in the Greek Theatre*, was published in 1989. He was also a translator and director, combining both skills and others in his marionette theatre with which he presented many Greek plays throughout England, America and Canada.

DON TAYLOR is a playwright and poet, and a director of plays in all the media, as well as a translator of Greek drama. His own stage plays include *The Roses of Evam, The Exorcism, Daughters of Venice, Retreat from Moscow* and *When the Barbarians Came*, as well as eleven original television plays – one of them, *The Testament of John*, the only TV play to have been written in verse – which he himself directed for BBC TV during the seventies and eighties, when the medium of television drama still existed as a separate form from film. Methuen also publishes two of his translations of Euripides, as well as his autobiographical account of his work with David Mercer in the sixties, *Days of Vision*; his poems, *A Prospect of Jerusalem*, are published by First Writes.

J. MICHAEL WALTON worked in the professional theatre as an actor and director before joining the University of Hull, where he is Professor of Drama. He has published four books on Greek theatre, *Greek Theatre Practice, The Greek Sense of Theatre: Tragedy Reviewed, Living Greek Theatre: A Handbook of Classical Performance and Modern Production* and *Menander and the Making of Comedy* (with the late Peter Arnott). He edited *Craig on Theatre* for Methuen and is Series Editor of Methuen Classical Greek Dramatists. He has translated plays by Sophocles, Euripides, Menander and Terence and is Director of the Performance Translation Centre in the Drama Department at the University of Hull.

Printed in the United Kingdom
by Lightning Source UK Ltd.
114177UKS00001B/220-225